of Agriculture Georgia. Dept., Thomas P Janes

The farmer's scientific manual

of Agriculture Georgia. Dept., Thomas P Janes

The farmer's scientific manual

ISBN/EAN: 9783337414443

Printed in Europe, USA, Canada, Australia, Japan

Cover: Foto ©Lupo / pixelio.de

More available books at **www.hansebooks.com**

THE FARMER'S

SCIENTIFIC MANUAL.

COMMISSIONER OF AGRICULTURE OF THE
STATE OF GEORGIA.

DEPARTMENT OF AGRICULTURE,
ATLANTA, GEORGIA.
1878.

INTRODUCTORY.

There has long existed among practical farmers a prejudice against the application of science to practical agriculture, or, as they have been pleased to call it, "book farming." This prejudice has not only retarded the progress of agriculture in the South, but has prevented farmers from seeking, through the medium of books and agricultural journals, the information so necessary to the most intelligent and profitable conduct of their peculiar business.

This prejudice has not only been to a large extent overcome in Georgia, but there is a manifest thirst for a knowledge of science as related to agriculture. There is a spirit of inquiry among the farmers of Georgia, excited to some extent by the publications of this Department, and manifested in the multitude of inquiries being received at this office, which renders the publication of the following work not only appropriate, but almost a necessity.

Empiricism has too long been the reproach of Southern agriculture.

It is the natural outgrowth of the necessary isolation of the owners of large landed estates.

There is no other occupation which naturally calls to its aid so many of the sciences as does that of agriculture.

Geology, mineralogy, chemistry, botany, zoology, meteorology, entomology, vegetable and animal physiology—all the natural sciences—reflect light upon agriculture as a pursuit, and hence the relations of these sciences to agriculture constitute appropriate fields of study for those who derive both pleasure and profit from the cultivation of the soil.

The farmer has to deal with soils and manures, with plants and animals, with insect friends and enemies, with temperature and moisture, and must use in his daily work various mechanical appliances, both simple and compound. The character, treatment, needs and mutual relations of all of these, should be understood by the advanced agriculturalist.

The object of this work is:

1st. To present, as briefly as is consistent with perspicuity, such information as will aid the farmers of Georgia in more thoroughly understanding the great leading principles which underlie the whole field of progressive agriculture.

2d. To stimulate the spirit of inquiry which now pervades the agriculturists of the State.

In the scope allotted to this pamphlet it is impossible to do more than whet the already growing appetite for knowledge, by presenting to the intellectual palate a few savory morsels, gleaned from the field of science, with the hope of stimulating such thought and research on the part of the farmers of Georgia, as will bring forth fruit both abundant and ripe, for future gleaners in the field of successful agriculture.

The losses annually sustained by the farmers of the State, in consequence of ignorance of the plainest teachings of agricultural science, afford ample justification for the publication of this MANUAL in which the difficult task is attempted of so popularizing the teachings of science, as applied to agriculture, that the unscientific, practical farmer may readily appropriate to his own use the results of scientific research.

No claim to originality is made. On the contrary, the material has been compiled from standard authors, condensed, simplified, and interwoven with illustrations and practical suggestions, applicable to our surroundings.

Those who wish to pursue still further the study of the subjects, that have been merely touched upon in this pamphlet, are referred to Scientific Agriculture—Dr. E. M. Pendleton; How Crops Grow and How Crops Feed—S. W. Johnson; Talks on Manures—Joseph Harris; Land Drainage—Klippart; and Structural and Systematic Botany —Professor Asa Gray.

CHAPTER I.

GENERAL CHEMISTRY.

Definition of Terms.

The natural sciences relate to the laws which govern the different departments of nature. The following are of especial interest to the agriculturist:

BOTANY.—The science of plants, embracing an account of their properties, structure, classification, and the laws which govern their growth and development.

ZOOLOGY.—The science of animals, their characteristics and relations to each other.

ENTOMOLOGY.—The science of insects.

MINERALOGY.—The science of minerals.

GEOLOGY.—The study of the earth, its age and formation; the character of its rocks and the soils derived from them; and the occurrence of its minerals.

METEOROLOGY.—The science of the atmosphere, and its various phenomena.

CHEMISTRY.—The study of the composition and properties of all material objects, including rocks, minerals, soils, plants and animals—everything, visible and invisible, in earth, water and air.

These will be treated in this work only so far as they relate to agriculture.

Chemistry teaches that all things in nature, animate and inanimate, solid, liquid and gaseous, are either simple substances, or are formed by the union of two or more simple substances, to each of which the name of *element* is given.

Each element is entirely distinct from the others, has its own peculiar properties and characteristics, and cannot be divided into two substances having distinct properties, To illustrate, lead is an element and cannot, by any known means, be divided into any other substances, while red lead is a compound of lead and oxygen. By the use of certain means the two elements can be completely separated.

Gold, silver, copper and tin are also elements.

There are only about sixty-six simple elements known to the chemist. Of these, and their various combinations, all matter, solid, liquid and gaseous, is composed.

When an element is found occurring naturally, and not combined with another, it is said to exist "free in nature."

Nearly all of the substances composing the vegetable, animal and mineral kingdoms, are combinations of two or more elements.

Matter is indestructible. The apparent destruction of a substance is merely the breaking up of its elements and the formation of new compounds.

Many of these elements have an attraction or affinity for each other; the rusting of iron is merely the union of iron with oxygen which exists in air and water. Heat, light and electricity aid the union of these elements.

It has been found that these elements are governed by laws in their union with each other, and that these laws, like those in other departments of nature, are uniform and constant in their operation.

One of these laws is, that elements always unite with each other in certain proportions by weight and volume; should there be an excess of one element present, it will remain uncombined.

The elements are divided into various classes, viz: those which exist as gases only, those which are liquid, and those which are solid.

Symbols.—Each element is designated by a letter, or letters, taken from its Latin name. When two letters are used, the first is a capital. Thus, the symbol of iron is Fe. Substances composed of two or more elements are designated by the grouping of the symbols of its different elements. Thus, hydrochloric or muriatic acid is composed of hydrogen and chlorine. The symbol of hydrogen is H., that of chlorine is Cl., hence the symbol of the acid is HCl. Very often one part, by weight, of an element unites with two or more parts of another. This is expressed by a figure placed at the right and a little below the symbol. For instance, H_2SO_4 represents sulphuric acid of commerce, which is composed of two parts of hydrogen, one of sulphur, and four of oxygen.

Below is a list of elements of the most practical value.

The list embraces the most important elements to be considered in this work. The symbol of each is given:

NON-METALLIC ELEMENTS.

Gases.
- Hydrogen..........H
- Oxygen............O
- Nitrogen...........N
- Chlorine..........Cl
- Fluorine...........F

Liquid—Bromine..........Br

Solids.
- Iodine..............I
- Sulphur............S
- Phosphorus........P
- Carbon............C
- Silicon............Si
- Boron.............B

METALLIC.

Alkaline.
- Potassium........K
- Sodium..........Na

- Calcium..........Ca
- Magnesium......Mg
- Aluminum.......Al
- Barium..........Ba
- Strontium........Sr
- Arsenic..........As
- Antimony.......Sb
- Chromium......Cr
- Cobalt..........Cr
- Copper.........Cu
- Gold............Au

- Iron.............Fe
- Lead............Pb
- Manganese.....Mn
- Mercury........Hg
- Nickel..........Ni
- Platinum.......Pl
- Silver...........Ag
- Tin.............Sn
- Titanium.......Ti
- Uranium.......Ur
- Zinc............Zn

In order that the reader may fully understand what is contained in this work, it is proper to define some of the terms which must necessarily be used in its progress.

An Experiment is a trial made under certain conditions to determine facts.

Analysis is the process of determining the composition of substances.

Qualitative Analysis is the determination of the elements contained in a substance, without reference to the quantity of each.

Quantitative Analysis is the determination of the amount (usually in per cent.) of each element contained in a substance.

A Mixture is a mechanical union of two or more substances—each still retaining its distinctive properties.

A Chemical Compound is the result of the chemical union of two or more substances, by which each loses its peculiar properties; the new substance having its own characteristics, different from those of the elements from which it is formed. Thus copper and sulphur rubbed together, ever so intimately, is still a *mixture*, since the grains of each may be distinguished by means of the microscope. If the mixture be heated, an entirely new substance will be produced having none of the peculiar properties of either sulphur or copper. This is a *chemical compound*.

An Acid has usually a sour taste, and will turn *blue litmus* (a vegetable matter) to a red color.

Bases.—This name is given to a class of substances which have the property of neutralizing acids and forming with them what are known as *salts*. They are divided into several classes, viz: *alkaline* (of which potash and soda are examples), which have the power of turning red litmus to a blue color, and have a strong caustic action upon fleshy tissue.

Alkaline Earths, which are not so strongly caustic; lime and magnesia are examples of these.

There is a third class, which show no alkaline property, except that of neutralizing acids.

The salts include a great number of chemical compounds formed by the union of acids and bases. They are designated by names derived from the acid which enters into the combination.

Those formed by the union of sulphuric acid with a base,

are called sulphates; with nitric acids, nitrates; with carbonic acid, carbonates, etc. They are generally neutral, possessing neither acid nor alkaline character.

The strength of the union of acids with bases varies, the acid possessing the stronger affinity for a given base, having the power of displacing the weaker, and taking its place in combination with the base.

This principle is utilized by the manufacturer of superphosphate to liberate phosphoric acid from its union with lime, and thus make it available for plant nutrition. When the pulverized phosphate of lime is treated with sulphuric acid, the sulphuric acid, having a stronger affinity for lime than the phosphoric acid, displaces a portion of the latter from its union with the lime, forming super-phosphate of lime, together with sulphate of lime.

About half of every acid phosphate, or commercial super-phosphate, is sulphate of lime.

Chemistry is divided into two general departments :

Organic, which treats of those compounds which have organized structure, whether vegetable or animal; and—

Inorganic, which includes all substances which have not organic structure, embracing the mineral kingdom, and such other compounds as have not been formed by life.

Inorganic compounds can be formed in the chemical laboratories, while organic are the result only of life in conjunction with other forces.

In the following pages the elements, with their chief compounds, will be briefly described, that the reader may obtain a general idea of those substances which, by their different combinations with each other, constitute the solid, liquid and gaseous substances of the world, so far as they may be deemed of interest to farmers.

Oxygen is a colorless, inodorous, tasteless gas. It exists free in the air, and has a powerful chemical affinity for other elementary substances. It is the most abundant and most widely distributed of all the elements. "In its free state (*mixed*, but not combined with nitrogen), it constitutes about one-fifth the bulk, and considerably more than one-fifth of the weight, of the atmosphere. In combination with hydrogen, it forms eight-ninths of all the water on the globe. In combination with silicon, calcium and other minerals, it enters largely into all the solid constituents of the earth's crust; silica, in its various forms of sand, common quartz, flint, etc—chalk, limestone and marble, and all the varieties of clay, containing about half their weight of oxygen. It is moreover found in all the tissues and fluids of all forms of animal and vegetable life, none of which can support existence independently of this element."

When substances are burned, the oxygen of the air forms chemical combinations with the substances consumed, one of the principal results of which is carbonic acid, which is also a result of slow combustion or decomposition—such as takes place in the decay of vegetable matter, the fermentation of the compost heap, and the digestion of food by animals. Animals inhale oxygen from the air, which, forming chemical union with the carbon of the food, and the impurities of the blood, is exhaled as carbonic acid.

When oxygen unites rapidly with other substances, the union is termed combustion; when the union takes place slowly, it is termed oxidation.

The rusting of iron is a familiar example of oxidation. The application of oil or other substance to the iron, to exclude the oxygen of the air, prevents this oxidation or rusting of the iron.

Hydrogen is a colorless, tasteless, inodorous, inflammable gas, which does not exist in a free state, being always combined with some other element.

The chief form in which it is found is in combination with oxygen in water.

If the two gases are mixed in the proportion of two of hydrogen to one of oxygen, they will not unite, but simply mix, mechanically. If, however, a spark of electricity or a lighted taper be brought in contact with them, there will be a violent explosion, as the result of the active chemical union of the two gases forming, first, watery vapor, which, being immediately condensed, causes a vacuum, into which air rushes with great force, producing the report.

Electricity will also decompose water, re-converting it into the two gases, which, if separated, will be found to be in the proportion of two of hydrogen to one of oxygen. The specific gravity of hydrogen, compared with that of common air, is as 69 to 1,000. It is sixteen times lighter than oxygen. In combination with nitrogen, it forms ammonia.

Water, nature's great solvent, is the most abundant constituent in all vegetation, and is indispensable, both to the germination and growth of plants, and to the existence of animal life. It is the necessary vehicle of all that portion of plant-food which is derived from the soil.

It is composed of oxygen and hydrogen, chemically combined in the proportion of two atomic weights of hydrogen, to one of oxygen. It exists, principally, as a liquid, but takes also a gaseous and solid form. It is liquid at ordinary temperature, boils at 212° F., and is rapidly converted into steam or vapor, evaporation taking place more gradually at lower temperatures, dependent upon motion and dryness of the surrounding medium.

It freezes at 32° F., becoming solid in the form of ice. Its greatest density is at 40° F., diminishing in density below that temperature until it becomes solid, and diminishing above with the increase of heat. The expansion in freezing or solidifying, which is an exception to a general law of nature, is a wise provision, which not only prevents the disastrous consequences which would result from an increase of density in solidification in cold climates, but serves a valuable purpose in agriculture: by its expansion in freezing, and the resulting pulverization of rocks and soils.

So great is the absorption and solvent power of water, that it is never found chemically pure in nature. It is obtained pure only by distillation, or the condensation of watery vapor or steam in closed vessels.

Rain-water is next in purity to that obtained by distillation. It contains no solid matter in solution, but absorbs, during its fall, gases from the air.

Well and spring-water contains not only absorbed gases, but mineral matter dissolved during its percolation through the earth. Lime, iron, sulphur, soda, magnesia, and other minerals, are thus dissolved, frequently in such quantities as to give taste, character, and even name, to the water.

The medicinal properties of the waters of springs are due to the mineral matters held in solution, and gaseous substances absorbed by them during their passage over mineral deposits in the earth.

The saltness of the water of the ocean, and lakes without outlets, is due to the evaporation of the water, leaving the salt in strong solution.

Nitrogen is a gas which constitutes about four-fifths of the air. It is colorless, tasteless, inodorous, and will neither support combustion nor respiration. Its chief use in the air seems to be to dilute the oxygen, with which it forms no chemical combination, but only a mechanical mixture. It enters largely into the composition of animal tissue, constituting what is known as "nitrogenous matter." Chemically combined with hydrogen, it forms ammonia, and with oxygen, nitric acid, both of which are valuable. fertilizers.

Salts resulting from the chemical combination of nitric acid with bases are called *nitrates*. With soda it forms nitrate of soda; with potash, nitrate of potash, both of which are used as fertilizers.

Though nitrogen is a necessary constituent of all plants, and though it exists in such large quantities in the air, it is never absorbed by plants from the air, or appropriated by their roots from the soil in the form of nitrogen, its supply in plant nutrition being derived exclusively from nitric acid and ammonia.

Ammonia.—This important compound, is a combination of nitrogen and hydrogen. It is formed by the decay, or decomposition, of organic matter, both animal and vegetable, containing nitrogen.

Ammonia gas is formed by the union of one atom of nitrogen with three of hydrogen. It has a very pungent and penetrating odor, and is strongly alkaline in property, instantly changing red litmus paper blue. With different acids it forms salts: with sulphuric acid it forms sulphate of ammonia; with nitric acid, nitrate of ammonia; with carbonic acid, carbonate of ammonia, etc.

It is called the "volatile alkali," because of its being easily driven off by heat, or displaced by other stronger alkalies and separated from its compounds. It is the most costly constituent of commercial fertilizers, and a necessary component of every fertile soil. It exists in very minute proportion, as free ammonia, in the atmosphere, from which it is absorbed as carbonate of ammonia by plants, or carried down to the soil by the rain, which absorbs it during its fall.

The principal sources from which ammonia for agricultural use is derived are dried blood, dried flesh, fish scraps, gas works, human excrement, (hoofs, horns and leather scraps, with exhaustive distillation), sewage and natural guano, or the accumulated deposits of marine birds. The principal natural sources on Georgia farms are cotton seed, stable manure, and the vines, roots and foliage of field peas. It performs a most important part in the growth of all vegetation, and is rapidly exhausted from soils under continuous clean culture.

Carbon is one of the most abundant elements in nature, forming nearly one-half of the material of the vegetable kingdom, and a very important constituent of many rocks, such as limestone, marble, etc. Its most prominent forms are mineral, coal, charcoal, graphite, soot, lamp-black, etc.

The diamond is pure, crystalized carbon. Coal consists of the remains of vegetable matter which once existed on the earth. It was formed by the agency of heat in the absence of oxygen of the air, in very much the same manner as charcoal is now produced, but on a larger scale. It has been found that to produce a foot of mineral coal requires from five to eight feet of dense vegetable matter, such as peat.

Bone-black or animal charcoal is made by burning bones in closed vessels, by which the organic matter of the bones is converted into charcoal. It is ground to a powder, and used in sugar refineries to remove the impurities from the sugar.

The crude sugar is dissolved, and the solution filtered through the bone-black, which absorbs the dark, impure matter, leaving a clear liquid, from which the pure white sugar is crystalized. After the bone-black has been used and "*revived*" several times it is treated with sulphuric acid, and the phosphate of lime, which it contains, is converted into super-phosphate of lime, and sold as a fertilizer.

The carbon contained in the cellular structure of plants is absorbed, both by the roots and leaves, in the form of carbonic acid, the oxygen of the compound being exhaled, and the carbon retained by the plant, and appropriated to its own use in building up its structure.

This structure is best seen in vegetable charcoal, in which the contents of the cells are burned out and only the framework left.

"*Peat* is an accumulation of half decomposed vegetable matter found in swampy places. It is produced mainly by a kind of moss, which gradually dies below as it grows above, and thus forms beds of great thickness; sometimes, however, plants may grow in the form of turf and decay, thus collecting a vast amount of vegetable debris. This gradually undergoes a change, and becomes a brownish, black substance, loose and friable in its texture, resembling coal." In some countries and cities peat is of value, and is used as fuel. For this purpose it is cut out in square blocks, dried in the sun and pressed. It contains about 60 per cent of carbon.

Muck is a variety of peat, containing more impurities and less fully carbonized. The largest bed of this material in Georgia is in Okefenokee Swamp, in the lower part of the State. It has there a thickness of several feet, and extends over many square miles.

Its value as a fertilizer is due mainly to its power of absorbing and retaining moisture and the ammonia of the atmosphere, and to the amount of mineral plant-food it may contain.

Humus is a general name applied to the partially decomposed vegetable matter embracing that contained in peat and muck, and as well as that resulting from the decay of green crops turned under. Its value, as well as the rapidity of the decomposition, depends upon the kind of vegetable matter from which it is formed. Its beneficial effects upon soils are due principally to its mechanical action in stiffening sandy and loosening clay soils; in its absorbtive and retentive power for moisture and ammonia; in its solvent power in rendering available mineral substances in the soil; and in supplying small amounts of plant-food liberated by the process of decomposition. The principal element evolved from humus is carbonic acid.

Carbonic Acid is a gas composed of carbon and oxygen, in the proportion of one atom of carbon to two of oxygen, and like other acids, is generally combined with other substances to form solids. For example, in chalk and marble we have this gas combined with lime. It, however, is also free in nature. It exists free in the atmosphere, and often in caves, mines, and old wells. It is colorless, has a pungent odor, and pleasant acid taste. It is heavier than the air, and will neither burn itself, nor support combustion, immediately extinguishing a burning taper immersed in it.

The gas may be generated by placing in a large jar about two teaspoonfuls of muriatic acid, and adding to it small pieces of limestone, marble, or a little carbonate of soda, until all effervescence ceases.

Effervescence shows that the gas is being liberated from its combination with the lime or soda. If, after a few minutes, a lighted taper is lowered into the jar, it will be extinguished.

The gas thus generated may be poured into another jar, settling to the bottom and displacing the air. If the lighted taper be now applied to the second jar, it will be again extinguished. This experiment proves that the gas is heavier than air, and that it will not support combustion. The presence of lime in marl may be detected in this way.

Carbolic acid gas is also formed when animal or vegetable matter is burned in the air.

The cause of the extinction of the flame when placed in this gas is that there is no free oxygen present. That which the gas contains has already as much carbon as it can take up, and hence the carbon which forms a part of the taper is left without any oxygen to combine with it to support combustion. Animal life immersed in this gas is immediately destroyed because of the exclusion of the oxygen necessary to respiration, independently of the poisonous effects of the gas. This gas is often found in old wells. and is then called choke-damp. Lives have been lost by descending into these without first lowering a burning taper to detect the presence of the gas.

A quantity of lime water, made from freshly slaked lime, thrown down the sides of the well will remove the gas by its combination with the lime.

Carbonic acid gas can, by pressure, be forced into liquids. When the pressure is removed, effervescence is produced by the escape of the gas.

The so-called soda water contains no soda; the effervescence being produced by the escape of the carbonic acid gas, which is forced by great pressure into water and held there by the soda fountain. As soon as the water is allowed to flow from the fountain into the glasses into which the syrups have been placed, the gas, being no longer under pressure, escapes, and produces the foaming.

The carbonic acid is generated on a large scale for soda fountains, by treating some form of carbonate of lime with sulphuric acid. The sulphuric acid combines with the lime, forming sulphate of lime, and setting the carbonic acid free. This is collected in a reservoir, and then forced into water, for use as the so-called soda water.

This effervescence is utilized by housewives in making bread. Yeast powders (which are composed of carbonate of soda and a little tartaric acid) or carbonate of soda and sour milk, are mixed with flour for making bread. By the action of heat the carbonic acid is set free, causing the expansion of the dough, or the "rising of the bread."

Carbonic acid gas is exhaled from the lungs of all animals. It is estimated that 140 gallons of this gas are thrown off from the lungs of a grown person in 24 hours. At this rate, the air in a close room, occupied by a number of persons, will soon become charged with this poisonous gas. The importance of proper ventilation is, therefore, apparent. The office of carbonic acid in plant nutrition, and the reciprocal supply and consumption of carbonic acid and oxygen, will be discussed in their appropriate places.

Combustion, in the popular definition of the term, is the decomposition of a substance, attended with light and heat. In the true sense of the term, these phenomena do not always attend it.

Combustion proper is the union of oxygen with another substance, forming a new compound.

Combustion may be rapid, as is the case when coal or

wood burns, or it may be gradual, as is seen in the slow decay of vegetable matter, the rusting of iron, etc. Vegetation, which contains much nitrogen, as pea or bean-vines or clover, decomposes or decays, by oxydation, much more rapidly than substances in which starch, cellulose, or other carbonaceous compounds, more largely predominate.

Oxygen is the great supporter of combustion in its widest sense.

The most combustible material will not burn without access to oxygen. Excluded from moisture and oxygen, vegetable matter will not decay, animal matter will not putrify. Water, thrown upon a flame, spreads over the burning substance, excludes the air with its contained oxygen, and the flame is extinguished. Fruits, vegetables and meats, heated to drive off the air, and to destroy the germs of fungoid ferments, and then hermetically sealed, escape decomposition and fermentation.

Oxygen has a tendency to unite with nearly every other substance, and, if the union is effected rapidly, light is generally, and heat always, produced. If the union takes place slowly, these phenomena are not perceptible, and the former does not generally occur.

Fermentation is a peculiar kind of decay or decomposition, which apparently acts spontaneously on animal or vegetable matter, "involving heat and a rapid evolution of gas." " There are several kinds of fermentation : vinous, acetous, lactic, etc. All three of these processes may take place at once in a mixture of cellulose, abuminoids, and sugar," (Pendleton's Scientific Agriculture). The primary cause of fermentation is the presence of microscopic fungi, which act as a ferment. The germs of these float in the air and germinate, when brought into contact with substances suited to their growth. They even exist in the pores of substances, in which they germinate, under favorable circumstances of warmth and moisture, and thus give rise to fementation, even in closed vessels.

When the process is once begun, oxygen is set free, which, again uniting with the elements of the body, facili- the progress of the phenomenon. Salt, applied to meat in sufficient quantity, penetrates the pores of the meat by asmodic action, and destroys the fungoid germs already in the meat, as well as those which it receives by deposition from the air.

Salt, applied to the compost heap in large quantities, has a tendency to retard both the fermentation and the result- ing decomposition of the mass. Applied in small quanti- ties, its action may be beneficial in preventing too rapid fermentation, and the consequent excess of heat, resulting in what is commonly known as "fire-fanging."

In the compost heap slow combustion [called by Liebig *eremecausis* (slow burning)], resulting from the union of free oxygen of the air with carbonacious substances, takes place in conjunction with internal fermentation.

The same occurs in the decay of leguminous plants, such as peas, clover, etc., which contain nitrogen in considera- ble quantity, when turned into the soil in a green state.

The souring of milk is supposed to be caused by the fungus *penicilium glaucum*, which, it is thought, converts the sugar of the milk into lactic acid. When the protect- ing covering, or skin of fruit, is broken or abraded, the flesh is attacked by microscopic fungi, which cause rapid decay.

Sulphur occurs naturally in some parts of the world, es- pecially near volcanoes, but it is more generally combined with some other elements. It is found combined with iron and copper in pyrite and copper pyrites, and also with lead and zinc as sulphides of these substances.

In commerce, sulphur has two forms: *brimstone*, or stick sulphur, and a fine powder known as *flowers of sulphur*. It burns readily with a blue flame, forming sulphurous acid gas, which has bleaching properties. The flowers of sulphur is successfully used in destroying fungi on both vegetable and animal life.

It exists in small quantities in both animal and vegetable structure, in combination with oxygen, as sulphuric acid.

Sulphuric Acid, the most important of all acids, is a combination of sulphur and oxygen. It is known as oil of vitriol, and its salts as vitriols. Sulphate of copper is known as blue vitriol, or blue-stone, which is used in solution to destroy the germs of the fungus which produces the smut in wheat. With iron, it forms sulphate of iron, known as green vitriol, or copperas, which is frequently used both as a preventive and remedy for disease in animals and fowls. It destroys fungi and animal parasites, and acts as a tonic by furnishing iron to the system.

Sulphuric acid is used very extensively in the arts and manufactures. Since Liebig discovered the solvent power of this acid on bone phosphate of lime, it has been, and is still, used very extensively to render the phosphoric acid contained in bone or mineral phosphate available as plant-food.

With lime, it forms sulphate of lime, or gypsum, which is also known in commerce as land plaster.

This salt is extensively used in agriculture, superphosphates containing from 40 to 50 per cent., as a result of the union of lime with the sulphuric acid used as a solvent. Sulphate of magnesia (Epsom salts), sulphate of soda (Glauber salts), sulphate of ammonia and sulphate of potash, are some of the most important salts of sulphuric acid.

It is found in small quantities in soils, animals and plants, being the only form in which sulphur can be taken up by the latter. It is supposed to act as a decomposing agent in the soil, rendering other substances available as plant-food, as well as supplying it directly.

Phosphorus is a soft solid, which, when freshly cut, has a bright metallic lustre. It takes fire when exposed to the air, burns with a bright flame and white fumes, and hence has to be kept in water. It cannot exist in the free state naturally, but is always found as phosphoric acid combined with some other element, forming the phosphate of that element.

Though phosphorus is extremely poisonous to all animal life, in combination with oxygen, as phosphoric acid, it is necessary to the growth and maturity of both plants and animals, forming an important constituent of the stems, leaves and seeds of plants, a large per cent. of the bones of animals, and is contained also in the other parts of the animal system.

As plants derive their mineral elements (except carbon) entirely from the soil, all fertile soils must necessarily contain a fair percentage of this important constituent.

Very many minerals contain phosphoric acid, and it is from their decomposition that soils naturally derive their supply.

The composition of bones, the best source of phosphoric acid for agricultural purposes, is as follows:

Animal matter	33 per cent.
Lime—phosphate	57 "
Lime—carbonate	8 "
Magnesium—phosphate	1 "
Other ingredients	1 "
	100

The chief sources of the phosphates of commerce are the minerals and rocks which contain them, and bones of animals, both fossil and fresh. The most noted beds of fossil bones and rocks are those near Charleston, S. C., which are now largely worked. The rocks and bones there found are the accumulations of the remains of marine animals which once inhabited the waters of the sea that covered that section ages ago. These beds are very extensive, and easily worked. The rocks and bones from them are crushed by machinery, ground to a powder, and subjected to the action cf sulphuric acid, by which the bone phosphate is converted into superphosphate of lime and sulphate of lime, and made available as plant food.

There is from 24 to 30 per cent. of phosphoric acid in the phosphate rock, from 10 to 15 per cent. of which is made available by treatment with sulphuric acid.

Bone Ash is obtained by burning bones with access to oxygen, by which the gelatinous material contained in them is burned out, leaving a friable mass which is readily acted upon by acids. In the absence of mills for crushing the bones, this is the cheapest and most effectual method of reducing them.

In the analysis of fertilizers, phosphoric acid is determined in three forms, viz: "soluble," "precipitated or reduced," and insoluble." The *first* is soluble in pure water, the *second*, in what is known as "soil water," or water having absorbed in it vegetable acids, ammonia, and carbonic acid, and is, therefore, available to plants. It is so-called from having been once in a soluble condition, but by time and other causes, has been changed, and its union with the lime made stronger.

The insoluble phosphoric acid is that which is still in its original condition, not having been acted upon by sulphuric acid, and soluble only in strong acids. It is not immediately available to plants.

In common insoluble phosphate of lime, there is a chemical union of three equivalents of lime to one of phosphoric acid. If, by the aid of sulphuric acid, two parts of this lime be taken up and converted into sulphate of lime (gypsum), there is left a soluble phosphate, in which the phosphoric acid is available as plant food.

Such a compound, in which there is phosphoric acid in a soluble or available form, is called a *superphosphate*.

The terms, monobasic, bibasic and tribasic phosphate of

lime represent the different forms in which the lime and phosphoric acid unite. In the first, the phosphoric acid unites with only one equivalent of lime, the second only two parts of lime, while the third, or tribasic, the usual form, unites with three parts. The tribasic is the form from which the superphosphate of commerce is manufactured.

Since the "precipitated," or "reduced," phosphoric acid is soluble in "soil water," it is considered of equal agricultural value with the "soluble," the two being classed together as AVAILABLE phosphoric acid. The insoluble portion of a superphosphate, derived from animal bone, (not charred,) is of greater value than that derived from phosphate rock, since it more readily becomes available to plants under the influence of acids and alkalies in the soil.

Silicon, in combination with oxygen, forms *silica*, and exists as such in a great variety of forms, such as quartz, flint, sand and rock crystal. As sand, it is found in all soils, forming the principal ingredient in some, and hardly perceptible in others.

Sand is formed by the disintegration of rocks containing quartz, and is spread over the earth's surface by the action of winds and water.

Silica exists in soils in two conditions:

1st. Insoluble silica, as pure grains of sand.

2d. Soluble silica, in combination with some other minerals or elements as silicates. Its chief compound is that of silicate of alumina, or clay. It enters largely into the composition of plants, especially so in the grasses and the common cane of our swamps.

Petrified wood is a *tree rock*, formed by the entrance of soluble silica into the cells of the wood, then hardening and displacing, or producing decay of, the vegetable matter, while retaining the woody form.

Silica is abundant in all soils, and though but a small per cent. of it is soluble, there is, usually, sufficient for the use of vegetation.

Potash is a combination of oxygen and a soft, white metal called *potassium*.

This metal cannot exist in the air, and, if thrown on water, burns with a bright purple flame.

Potash is obtained by leaching the ashes of hickory, oak and other hardwood trees in the form of lye, from which the water may be evaporated, leaving crude potash. This, when somewhat purified, is called pearl ash, which is a compound of carbonic acid and potash, or carbonate of potash. Potash is spoken of as caustic, on account of its strong corrosive action on the skin. It is one of the strongest alkalies, and forms salts with all acids.

It is an essential ingredient of plants, from which it is obtained in the form of carbonate of potash, though it does not exist in that form in plants, but is there usually united with some vegetable acid.

Its chief source in soils is from feldspathic and micarious rocks, and the decomposition of vegetable matter.

Its principal commercial source is the kainit, which is mined at Strassfurt, Prussia, the composition of which is as follows :

Sulphate of potassa.................. from 28 to 32 per cent
Sulphate of magnesia ....from 14 to 20 per cent
Chloride of magnesium...............from 4 to 5 per cent
Sulphate of lime............ ....from 10 to 12 per cent
Chloride of sodium.....................from 35 to 40 per cent

This deposit was struck at a depth of from 480 to 812 feet. The thickness of the bed is still unknown, though it has been pierced over 1,000 feet. It extends over an area of twenty-five German miles in length.

Chloride of Potassium, known also as muriate of potash, is found near Strassfurt, in Prussia, where it exists in a bed of clay, overlying a bed of rock salt, 100 feet in thickness. Nearly one-fourth of the weight of this clay is chloride of potassium. It is considered the cheapest, though probably not the best, source of potash for agricultural purposes.

Kainit is being extensively used, as a source of potash, by manufacturers of commercial fertilizers.

Nitrate of Potash, or saltpetre, is another form in which it is used for agricultural purposes, but it is more expensive, on account of its combination with nitrogen. It is obtained from soils in India, and from "nitre beds" in Europe, where refuse lime and animal manures are thrown up in loose heaps, exposed to the air, but protected from rain. It is allowed to remain for several years, when water is leached through it, and then collected and evaporated, leaving the crystallized nitre.

Soda, like potash, is a compound of oxygen, with a soft, white metal, called *sodium*, which has to be kept under naptha-oil to prevent its catching fire. It also burns on water.

Soda is caustic in its action, and, when combined with carbonic acid, is known as carbonate of soda, or sal-soda.

In nature, soda occurs chiefly in common salt, or chloride of sodium.

The waters of the ocean contain so much of this salt as to make them unfit for drinking purposes.

The chief source of our salt supply is in the evaporation of the sea water, which is carried on extensively along the shores of the Mediterranean Sea. Each gallon of water contains about four ounces of salt.

Immense beds of salt occur in some parts of the world, and afford another source of supply. This is called rock salt, from its massive rock-like appearance. It is quarried and crushed to different degrees of fineness.

Large quantities of salt are also obtained by evaporating the waters of salt springs, which occur at Syracuse in New York, in Western Pennsylvania, Ohio, West Virginia, Michigan, and some of the Western States and Territories.

There were produced in the United States, in 1870, 17,606,105 bushels of salt, valued at $4,818,229.

When the evaporation takes place rapidly, the crystals

are small, as in fine table salt; and when very slowly, a much coarser kind, called *bay salt*, is produced. That produced by slow evaporation is much stronger than the finer kind, and is generally used for preserving meat and fish in brine.

From common salt is obtained all of the other compounds of soda, by certain processes, which it is not necessary to describe here.

Carbonate of soda is used very extensively in the manufacture of glass, soap, etc.

Sulphate of soda, or Glauber's salts, as medicine.

Chillian saltpetre, or nitrate of soda, as a fertilizer.

Bicarbonate of soda is used in connection with sour milk in making bread.

Lime is a compound of oxygen with a metal called *calcium*, and, while its salts are generally known as those of lime, yet the term calcium is often used; thus, sulphate of lime is the same as calcium sulphate.

As with the metals, potassium and sodium, the metal calcium is of little use, and is kept, like them, out of contact with air or water.

Lime exists, in nature, in many forms, entering into the composition of nearly all rocks.

Caustic, or *quick* lime is made by heating limestone or any other carbonate of lime.

The heat drives off the carbonic acid gas, and leaves a hard and dry rock. By long exposure to air, this crumbles, or is "air-slaked," by the absorption of moisture and carbonic acid from the air; but, if water be poured on it, the rock takes it up so vigorously that great heat is evolved, and the lime immediately slaked.

In slaking, it is found that 28 pounds of lime will absorb 9 pounds of water, and swell to three times its original bulk.

Carbonate of lime occurs abundantly in limestone, marble, chalk, marl-shells, etc.

Marls are usually composed of clay, with shells, more or less crushed, imbedded in it.

Their value depends, principally, upon the per cent. of carbonate of lime which they contain. Some, however, contain potash and phosphoric acid. An application of marl to land, in conjunction with coarse manure, or green vegetable matter, materially improves, both the mechanical condition and chemical constitution of light and heavy soils.

Carbonate of lime is, to some degree, soluble in water which contains carbonic acid, and, hence, in localities where these limestones exist, there are many springs whose waters, passing over the rock, dissolve some of the limestone, and are known as "limestone springs." This limestone water, when evaporated to dryness, leaves a deposit of lime. This is seen in kettles and boilers, in which this water is heated, as an incrustation on the bottoms and sides. In boilers, connected with steam engines, this has has to be guarded against, since the crust thus formed becomes, eventually, thick enough to prevent access of the water to the iron, which becomes red-hot, or burns, and, in either case, results in the bursting of the boiler.

In limestone caves, the water, saturated with lime, drips through the rock above, and, by exposure to air, soon evaporates, leaving a small deposit of lime. This process is continued by successive drops of water saturated with lime, each leaving its small deposit, until, after a long period, a conical mass is formed, with its base attached to the roof of the cave. This is called a *stalactite*. When the water falls to the floor, and builds up from below, the rounded mass is called a *stalagmite*. The two often grow toward each other, and unite into a column.

Lime forms the usual salts, with acids; with sulphuric acid it forms sulphate of lime, or gypsum. This exists in nature in various forms. The massive variety is known as *alabaster*; is very soft, and can be cut into rings, boxes and ornaments.

Gypsum is known agriculturally as "land plaster," and, for some crops, is highly valued as a fertilizer.

"*Plaster of Paris,*" is made by heating gypsum to such a temperature that all the water will be driven off, and a white powder left.

This has the power of absorbing water and becoming very hard. It is used in making casts and moulds, and in cementing articles. For this purpose a thick paste is made of it with water, and used immediately, allowing it to stand for some hours, until perfectly hard.

Phosphate of Lime, which is, as before stated, a compound of phosphoric acid with lime, forms the chief constituent of bones, and is a valuable fertilizer; especially when reduced to the condition of super-phosphate, or soluble phosphate, by treatment with sulphuric acid.

Chloride of Lime forms the well-known bleaching powder of commerce. Its effect is limited to vegetable stains and colors, and is due to the chlorine.

Magnesium is a white, light metal, which burns in the air with a very bright light.. It is largely used in photography, for which purpose it is prepared in the form of wire or tape.

Magnesia; or Oxide of Magnesium, is found in many rocks, especially in dolomite or magnesian limestone. It forms an important constituent of agricultural plants, occurring in considerable quantity in the seeds of cereals, ranking next to potash and phosphoric acid in quantity. "In the ash of small grain cereals it ranges from 8 to 12 per cent., and in Indian corn runs up as high as 14.6 per cent." —(Pendleton.)

It exists in sufficient quantity in most soils, but its application in small quantities is desirable on lands that have been long cultivated.

Aluminum is the lightest metal known.

Its *oxide, alumina,* occurs naturally in large quantities, forming as a silicate, the clay of our soils. While it does not contribute materially to the direct nutrition of plants, its mechanical influence upon the soil, and its absorbtive and retentive power for moisture, ammonia and other fertilizing matters, make it an important agent in agriculture. When pure, it is extensively used in manufactures. The pure, white alumina, called " kaolin," is found in considerable quantities in Georgia, and is being used in the manufacture of earthenware.

Corundum, also found in Georgia, another form of pure alumina, possesses a high value as a polishing material. The *sapphire, emerald, topaz* and *ruby* are also forms of alumina.

The paint, *yellow or red ochre*, is clay, colored with iron.

Alum is a double salt of sulphuric acid with alumina and potash. It is used in dyeing, to unite with the coloring matter, and fix it in the fibre of the cloth.

Chlorine is a gas occurring only in combination with other elements, chief among which is sodium, forming common salt, chloride of sodium. The chief importance of chlorine is in its bleaching effects. For this purpose, it is combined with lime, or calcium and oxygen, forming chloride of lime, or bleaching powder. Vegetable colors only are effected by it, and the presence of water is necessary. It is also largely used as a disinfectant, to remove poisonous vegetable gases. Chlorine, combined with hydrogen, forms hydrochloric, or muriatic acid.

Iron occurs most abundantly diffused over the earth, being found, in some form, in plants, minerals, soils, waters, and even in the blood of animals. Soils are colored with it, and it even floats in fine particles in the atmosphere.

That it is the most useful of all metals, and possesses properties exactly suited to the wants of man, is not questioned.

Pure metallic iron is not found occurring naturally. Its

purest natural form is in meteorites, in which it is alloyed with nickel.

The ores from which iron is chiefly obtained are the magnetic oxide, and red and brown hematites (oxides), which, in some localities, are found in great masses. The iron is easily reduced from these, by heating, at a very high temperature, with coal and limestone, in furnaces made for the purpose, The impurities of the iron remain in the *slag*, the oxygen is driven off, and the melted iron, containing carbon, collects at the bottom of the furnace, and is run off in the form of *pig iron*.

The usual forms of iron in use are cast, wrought, and steel.

Cast Iron contains much carbon, and is merely pig iron remelted and run into moulds made in the desired form. These moulds are made of a mixture of sand and other material.

Wrought Iron is made from cast, or pig, iron by burning out some of the carbon, and drawing out the iron between huge rollers, into rods, bars, or plates. Thus treated, it becomes fibrous in structure, and will not break so easily as the cast iron. It is hardened by cooling rapidly, and softened by cooling slowly.

Steel contains more carbon than wrought iron, and has less than cast, and is more difficult to manufacture. Its value depends upon its tempering qnality.

Case-hardened is a term applied to those articles, such as cheap knives, whose surface only is steel, while the interior of the blade is soft iron. As soon as the steel surface is worn off, the soft iron is exposed, and will take no edge.

Welding.—Wrought iron and steel become soft without melting, at certain temperatures, and two pieces may, by hammering, be united together. That they may unite perfectly, it is necessary that their surfaces be free from iron rust, or oxide of iron, which is formed in heating, and hence some substance is used to protect them. Borax is generally used for this purpose, because of its cheapness.

Galvanized Iron is merely iron covered with a thin coating of zinc, which prevents it from rusting. Telegraph wire is so protected.

Iron Pyrites, a very common mineral, is a combination of sulphur and iron. It is brittle, and has a bright, yellow appearance, so nearly like that of gold that it is often called "fools' gold," from the fact that many persons have been deceived by it. The test is simply roasting the powdered material in a shovel, when the odor of burning sulphur will be recognized, and the mass will change color. One of its principle uses is in the manufacture of sulphuric acid.

Sulphate of Iron, known as copperas, or green vitriol, is made from iron pyrites. It is used in dyeing, making ink and medicinally.

Spring Waters are often impregnated with iron, which has been dissolved by the water while passing over beds of ore in the earth. On exposure to the air the dissolved iron is oxidised, and forms a scum on the surface, or a yellow deposit on the sides and bottom of the spring. These are called *chalybeate springs*, and have valuable tonic properties.

Arsenic and Antimony occur in nature in several forms. Their use is chiefly in medicine.

"*Scheele's Green*" is a poisonous compound of arsenic and copper, which is in extensive use. It forms most of the bright, green colors of wall paper. Its use should be avoided, since metallic arsenic and another extremely poisonous form of arsenic is set free, and floats in the atmosphere of rooms covered with such paper.

"*Paris Green*," another salt of arsenic with copper, has been used to kill the cotton worm and potato bug. It, too, is a dangerous substance.

The usual form of *antimony* used in medicine is *tartar*

emetic, which is formed by its union with potash and tartaric acid.

Barium occurs usually as sulphate of barium, when it is called *heavy spar*, because of its weight. It is largely used to adulterate white lead.

Bromine is a dark, reddish liquid, of no general importance, except in combination with potassium, as "bromide of potassium.

Bromide of magnesium and sodium is found in certain mineral springs.

Chromium is a metal occurring chiefly with iron and oxygen, as chrome iron ore. It is used not only in the formation of several salts of the drug stores, as chromate and bi-chromate of potash and of lead, but very largely in the green coloring matter known as chrome green. Greenbacks are colored with it.

Cobalt is a metal of no special importance. The name has sometimes been given to a fly poison, which is very dangerous, being chiefly metallic arsenic.

Copper is found as a metal in nature, but more frequently combined with some other element, as oxygen and sulphur. It enters into many of the useful alloys, chief among which is brass. Its important salt is the sulphate or bluestone.

Verdigris, or the acetate of copper, which is poisonous, is formed when fruits or acid vegetables are boiled in copper vessels. Copper forms other salts with different acids.

The test for copper in its ore is to bring it into solution with nitric acid and add ammonia. The solution will appear deep blue, should copper be present.

Lead is usually found as galena, which is a combination of lead and sulphur. It is obtained pure from its ore by means of furnaces. It is used not only pure, but in a large number of alloys. It is slightly soluble in well and spring waters.

Litharge and red lead are two different oxides of lead. The latter is used chiefly in glass making.

Sugar of lead is its combination with acetic acid. White lead is the carbonate, manufactured largely for use in paints.

Mercury, known as quicksilver, is a heavy liquid which is not often found except in combination with sulphur. It freezes at 40 degrees below zero. It is used largely in various meteorlogical instruments, in extracting gold and silver from their ores, and for silvering mirrors. *An Amalgam* is a union of mercury with other metals. In medicine, mercury is contained in "blue mass," in the metallic form very finely disseminated through the mass; in combination with chlorine, as calomel and corrosive sublimate.

Manganese is one of the elements found in all soils, though generally in very small quantities. It is largely used in various manufactures.

Nickel occurs combined with other elements. Its chief use is in the alloys of German silver.

Platinum is a comparatively rare and valuable metal, used principally in chemical laboratories. It can only be melted at the very highest heat, viz: that produced by burning oxygen and hydrogen together.

Silver is found both pure and combined with other minerals. It is used principally in alloys with copper, as in coins and articles of plate. Its most important salt is the nitrate of silver, known as lunar caustic when in sticks.

Indelible Ink, for marking linen, is made of this salt.

Tin has been found in but few localities, always combined with another element. It is used largely in the arts for covering iron plates.

The "sheets of tin," of which ordinary tin vessels are made, are only thin sheets of iron covered with a coating of tin to protect them from rusting.

It is also used in various alloys, as pewter, Britannia metal, plumber's solder, bronze, etc.

Zinc is an abundant and useful metal, which is found only combined with sulphur and other elements.

It is used as a coating for iron, which is then said to be galvanized. It is also used with alloys.

CHAPTER II.
PLANTS.

The Structure and Offices of Their Different Parts—Roots —Stems—Leaves, etc.

As the business of the agriculturalist involves, mainly the cultivation of plants for the purpose of facilitating the development of particular parts of the vegetable organism, intended for his own use, or that of his domestic animals, it becomes a matter of prime importance that he should understand their nature, structure, necessities, methods of development, and their relations to the soil and atmosphere, upon which they are dependent for existence and growth.

Successful agriculture secures the greatest development of the most useful parts of cultivated plants, at the least practicable cost.

An intimate knowledge of the normal conditions of plant development and plant nutrition is necessary to successful agriculture in its full sense.

Plants are complex organic structures, composed of roots, stems and leaves, each of which contributes to the fulfillment of their destiny, viz : the production of seed or fruit.

Roots, generally, serve the double purpose of fixing the plant firmly in the soil and supplying all of the food not derived from the atmosphere. In some they serve, also, as a store-house of food for future plants. Roots increase in size in the same manner as stems, but elongate by an entirely different process.

The commonly accepted theory of spongeoles at the *extremities* of growing roots, through which nourishment is absorbed, is rejected by the best modern authorities on vegetable physiology, after careful microscopic investigation.

Prof. Gray says: "The root, however, does not grow from its very apex, as is commonly stated; but the new formation (by continued multiplication of cells) takes place just behind the apex, which consists of an obtusely conical mass of older cells. As these wear away, or perish, they are replaced by the layer beneath; and so the advancing point of the root consists, as inspection plainly shows, of older and denser tissue than the portion just behind it.

"The point of every branch of the root is capped in the same way. It follows, that the so-called *spongeoles* or, *spongelets*, of the roots, or enlarged tips of delicate forming tissue, have no existence.

"Not only are there no special organs of this sort, but absorption evidently does not take place, to any considerable extent, through the rather firm tissues of the very point itself."

This "root-cap," the cells of which are filled with air, instead of sap, protects the tender formative tissue, and facilitates the extension of the root in the soil.

Besides the forming tissue, near the extremities of the proper roots, there are numerous "root-hairs" on the new parts of the roots. These are the active agents in the absorption of food from the soil.

Roots do not increase in size so rapidly as stems, nor are they so regular in their formation. They differ, also, from stems in increasing in length only at their extremities, while stems grow both by accretion at the end by the formation of new buds, and by elongation of the tender parts.

The extreme attenuation of the advancing root greatly facilitates its insinuation into the soil, while it enables it to change its course readily, when obstacles prevent further progress in a given direction.

Roots require, for their growth and normal development, warmth, moisture and oxygen, to enable them to perform their functions.

Different plants require different degrees of warmth and moisture. Cotton thrives best under a high temperature, and requires a moderate degree of moisture, while corn requires less warmth and more moisture.

Deep and thorough preparation, and drainage of the soil, facilitate the removal of surplus water in wet seasons; enable roots to penetrate more deeply, in search of moisture, during drouths; admit atmospheric air, from which the soil derives moisture by condensation of watery vapor, and oxygen and carbonic acid, both for the immediate use of the roots, and for the decomposition and preparation of inert substances for plant-food.

The character and form of the roots, even of the same plant, will vary according to the degree of pulverization of the soil, and the distribution of the plant-food, as well as the fertility of the soil. In poor soil, the roots are more attenuated, and much longer, than in fertile.

In the latter, they branch and ramify much more extensively, permeating every part of the soil adjacent to the plant, but acquiring less length in the individual root. The absorbing surface is, therefore, greater in fertile than in poor soils.

Roots seem to seek manure. A mass of well decomposed manure, placed near the plant, will be found filled with a multitude of fibrous roots; but this is probably due to the xtra development resulting from the nutrition derived from the manure, while those in parts of soil deficient in plant-food either fail to develop, or perish. There are many facts, however, which indicate a self-determining power of directing their course in search of both food and moisture. If manure is placed around a beet seed, at a depth of only a few inches, with sterile soil below, the lateral roots will enlarge, and extend themselves into the manure, while there will be no fleshy root below; hence, to produce long, well developed roots, the manure should be placed at considerable distance below the surface.

A cotton plant which germinates during a drouth, when the surface soil is dry, will have no lateral roots above the point at which it reaches moist soil ; one that germinates when the surface soil is saturated with moisture will have lateral roots within half an inch of the surface. Again, in times of drouth, the roots will be found penetrating deeply in search of moisture.

The roots of our cultivated plants may be divided into two general classes, namely : *tap-roots*, and *crown* or *lateral roots*.

All plants whose seeds readily divide into two parts in

Fig. 1.

germination, forming two seed leaves—called *aicatyledonous plants*—and whose stems increase by additions to the out side—*exogenous plants*—have, at first, single descending *tap roots*, which extend vertically into the soil.

From these, lateral roots branch out with some regularity, if the soil is in a finely pulverized and open condition, but usually irregularly, on account of the resistance of the soil. These lateral roots branch and ramify in the surface soil, in search of food, which they absorb through the tender parts of the roots proper, and the "root hairs" which cluster along its sides. The *tap-root* seems to serve the double purpose of firmly fixing the plant in the soil, and of absorbing mineral food and moisture from the sub-soil.

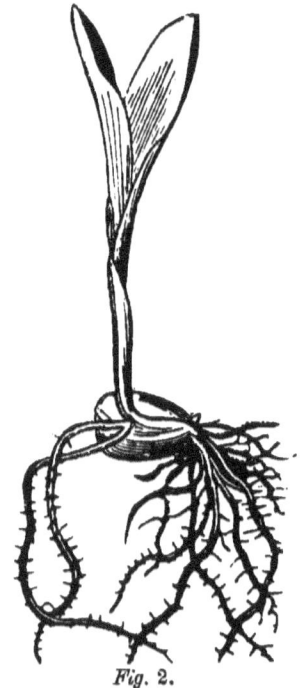

Fig. 2.

The upper portion of the tap-root of some plants, as the carrot, beet, turnip, etc., enlarge, under cultivation, into fleshy storehouses of food for the production of the seed-stalk the second year. They are bi-ennial plants. Other plants, such as the sweet potato, store the food for future plants, by the enlargement of their lateral roots.

Fig. 1 represents a young dicatyledonous plant at different stages of its growth soon after germination, illustrating the formation of both stem and root.

Those plants whose seeds do not divide readily into two equal or nearly equal parts, which put forth a single leaf at germination, and grow from the inside—*monocatyledonous plants*, or *endogens*—have no tap-root, but put forth a number of roots—crown-roots—at the base of the stem. (Fig. 2.) The grasses, including small grain and corn, are examples of this class.

Notwithstanding the plants have no tap-root, under favorable circumstances, their roots descend to great depths. The roots of wheat have been found at the depth of from three to four feet in light sub-soil. Those plants whcih have more than two cotyledons are called *polycotyledons*. Fig. 3 represents the magnified seed of the pine, and the young plant.

Roots, as well as plants, are further divided into annual, bi-ennial and perennial.

Aquatic and aerial roots, being of no special interest to the farmer, are omitted.

When we consider the fact that plants are entirely dependent upon their roots for their supply of all of the mineral elements of their food, except carbon, and for their entire supply of water, their importance to the agriculturist demands careful study of their nature, needs and methods of development.

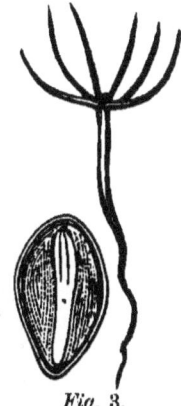

Fig. 3.

The absorptive power of the root seems to reside in the newly formed parts, near the extremities of the principal roots, but more particularly in the "root hairs," which thickly cover the new portions as they advance, and disappear as the surface grows hard and becomes covered with thick bark. (See Fig. 4.)

The tender, newly formed extremities of the roots are also destitute of these "root hairs," as may be observed by a close inspection of the roots of a plant soon after germination. The parts covered with "root hairs" will be found closely enveloped in fine earth, while the rest will be bare.

The force with which active roots absorb the water of the soil, with the plant-food in solution, is very great, ex—

erting a pressure on every part of the interior of the plant. It varies in different plants, and in the same plant under different circumstances.

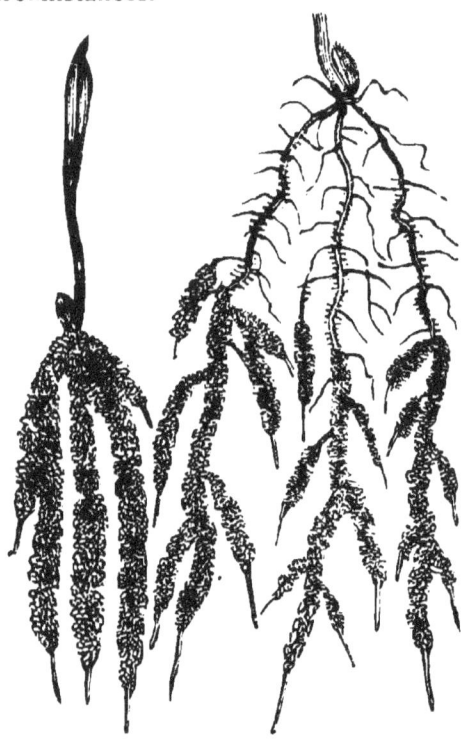

Fig. 4.

It is greatest when the roots are in a state of most rapid development, and under favorable circumstances as to supply of warmth and moisture, but manifested most plainly just before growth commences in spring, as seen in the sugar maple, grape vine, etc.

There are three forces which take part in the action of the roots of plants in the performance of their functions of absorption of crude plant-food, and the simultaneous assimilation of the same in adding to their absorbing surface. These are *osmose*, acting through the cellular system; adhesion, manifested in capillary attraction, stimulated by evaporation, and auxiliary to osmose; and vital force, which, together with chemical action, produces the resultant vegetable organism, beginning with the germ of the seed, and returning in annual cycles to the seed again. Osmose and capillary forces supply the material; vital force and chemical action utilize them.

Osmose is a general term applied to the interchange of liquids of different densities through organic, membranous partitions, and embraces both *endosmose*, the inward, and *exosmose*, the outward flow of the liquid.

Professor Gray says:

"*Endosmose* and *exosmose* are names given by Dutrochet (a French physiologist), to a physical process of permeation and interchange, which takes place in fluids according to the following law, briefly stated: When two liquids of unequal density are separated by a permeable membrane, the lighter liquid, or the weaker solution, will flow into the denser or stronger, with a force proportioned to the difference in density (endosmose); but, at the same time, a smaller portion of the denser liquid will flow out into the weaker (exosmose).

"Thus, if the lower end of an open tube closed with a thin membrane, such as a piece of moistened bladder, be introduced into a vessel of pure water, and a solution of sugar in water be poured into the tube, the water from the vessel will shortly be found to pass into the tube, so that the column of liquid it contains will increase in height to an extent proportionate to the strength of the solution. At the same time, the water in the vessel will become slightly sweet; showing that a small quantity of syrup has passed through the pores of the membrane into the water without, while a much larger portion of water has entered the tube. The water will continue to enter the tube, and a small portion of the syrup to leave it, until the solution is reduced to the same strength as the liquid without.

"If the same solution be employed both in the vessel

and the tube, no transferrence or change will be observed; but, if either be stronger than the other, a circulation will be established, and the strong solution will be increased in quantity until the two attain the same density. If two different solutions be employed, as, for instance, sugar or gum within the tube, and potash or soda without, a circulation will in like manner take place, the preponderance being *toward* the denser fluid, and in a degree proportionate to the difference in density."

This process goes on through the entire cellular system of the plant, commencing with the root, and acting through millions of cells during the ascent of the sap to the leaves, where evaporation condensing the fluids in the cells at the surface of the leaves, facilitates both osmose and capillary attraction; vital force, in the meantime, aided by chemical action, appropriating in the process of assimilation the prepared food for building up the various parts of the vegetable organism.

The roots of plants and trees generally correspond, to some extent, in form with the part above ground. The pine has a continuous stem extending to the top of the tree; the root also extends vertically into the ground to a great depth, unless modified by impenetrable obstacles in the sub-soil. The dogwood and red bud spread out into fan-like lateral branches, having no continuous central stem; the roots have a corresponding arrangement, all being distributed near the surface of the ground, with no tap-root. Most biennial and perennial plants which are outside growers (exogens) have tap-roots, while very few inside growers (endogens) have them. The form of plants may be somewhat modified by pruning the roots. Advantage is taken of this principle by the gardener in transplanting cabbage, lettuce and other plants which are desired to form compact heads. When transplanted, the tap-root is either broken or cut off.

Root development is most active and necessary while the plant is rapidly developing new growth, and preparing to produce fruit, or seed; hence the necessity, especially in our climate, of disturbing the roots as little as possible during the cultivation of the plant in summer.

Our cotton and corn crops are often seriously injured by deep plowing while the plants are in full process of development, and especially during the fruiting season, when every source of supply is needed to support them. Root pruning may prove beneficial when the plant is young, in causing additional ramification of fibrous branch roots, and thus inducing a greater production of fruit, as the result both of the pruning and of the *loosening of the soil;* but the absorbing surface of the roots should not be curtailed while the plant is *producing fruit, nor for a reasonable length of time before this process is commenced.*

Stems serve as a medium of communication between the roots and leaves of the plant, and as a support for the flowers, fruit, or seed, to which their functions are generally subordinate—since the *natural* end of all plants is the production of seed. Many plants, however, are cultivated by the agriculturist and horticulturist for the sake of the enlarged fleshy root or tuber, the tender stem, the succulent or fragrant leaves, the pulpy covering of the seed (called fruit), the saccharine or gummy juice of the stem, the hardened, timber-producing stem, the flower (prized either for its beauty or fragrance), the fibre attached to the seed, or forming the inner bark of the stem, for the medicinal properties of root, stem, bark, leaves or buds, or as food for insects useful to man.

When seeds germinate, the roots first make their appearance, and form what is termed the "descending axis," soon to be followed by the stem, or the ascending axis.

"In the seed, the stem exists is a rudimentary state, associated with undeveloped leaves, forming a *bud.* The stem always proceeds, at first, from a bud, during all its growth is terminated by a bud at every growing point, and only ceases to be thus tipped when it fully accomplishes its growth by the production of seed, or dies from injury or disease."

"In the *leaf-bud* we find a number of embryo leaves, or leaf-like scales, in close contact with each other, but all attached at the base to a central conical axis (Fig. 5). The opening of the bud consists in the lengthening of this axis, which is the stem, and the consequent separation of the leaves from each other. If the rudimentary leaves of a bud are represented by a nest of flower-pots, the smaller placed within the larger, the stem may be signified by a rope of India rubber, passed through the holes in the bottom of the pots. The growth of the stem may be shown by stretching the rope, whereby the pots are brought away from each other, and the whole combination is made to assume the character of a fully developed stem, bearing its leaves at regular intervals; with these important differences, that the portions of the stem nearest the root extend more rapidly than those above them, and the stem has within it the material and the mechanism for the continual formation of new buds, which unfold in successive order.

Fig. 5.

"In the accompanying cut (Fig. 6), which represents the two terminal buds of a lilac twig, is shown, not only the external appearance of the buds, which are covered with leaf-like scales, *imbricated*, like shingles on a roof; but, in the section, are seen the edges of the undeveloped leaves attached to the conical axis. All the leaves and the whole stem of one summer's growth thus exist in the bud in plan and in miniature. Subsequent growth is but the development of the plan.

Fig. 6.   "In the *flower-bud* the same structure is

manifest, save that the rudimentary flowers and fruit are enclosed within the leaves, and may often be seen plainly on cutting the bud open." (Johnson's How Crops Grow.)

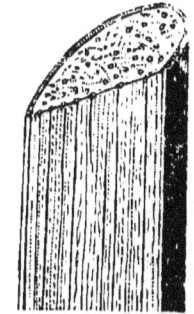

The stem as naturally ascends, seeking light and air, as the root descends and spreads in the soil, in search of food.

Plants are divided, as regards their stems, into two general classes: *endogens* (Fig. 7), or *monocatyledonous* plants, and exogens, or dicatyledonous plants (Fig. 8).

Endogens embrace all of those plants whose stems grow from the inside, which, at germination, have only one seed-leaf, and which put forth a number of roots from the base of the seed.

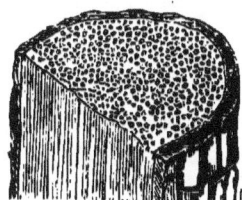

Fig. 7.

To this class belong the cereals, grasses, palms, etc. Another peculiarity of these plants is, that the bark cannot be separated from the wood, and that the outside hardens while the centre is yet soft.

Fig. 8.

Exogens embrace those plants whose stems increase by successive layers or rings next to the bark, have at germination two seed-leaves, and extend into the soil a vertical tap-root, from which lateral roots branch out with more or less regularity, dependent somewhat upon the pulverulent condition of the surrounding soil. A large majority of plants, shrubs and trees is embraced in this class, especially in higher latitudes.

The stems of endogens are composed of "separate bundles, or threads, of woody fibre, etc., running through the cellular system, without apparent order; and presenting, on the cross sections, a view of the divided ends of these threads, in the form of dots diffused through the whole; but with no distinct pith, and no bark which is at any time readily separable from the wood."—GRAY. (See Fig. 7.)

During their growth, the new woody matter is not formed by additions to the outside of the stem next to the bark, but "is intermingled with the old, or deposited towards the centre, which becomes more and more occupied with the woody threads as the stem grows older ; and the increase in diameter, so far as it depends upon the formation of new wood, generally takes place by the distension of the whole."—GRAY.

Exogens, or *outside growers*, (see Fig. 8) are composed of a multitude of closed cells, within which the vital principle acts in building up the structure of the plant. "In them and by them its products are elaborated, and all its vital processes carried on."

"A young, living, vitally active cell consists—1st. Of the membrane or permanent (cell) wall; 2d. Of a delicate mucilaginous film, lining the wall, called by Mohl the *primordial utricle;* 3d. Most commonly the centre of the cell, and sometimes the greater part of the cavity, is occupied by the *nucleus,* a soft solid, or gelatinous body; and 4th. The space between the nucleus and the lining membrane is filled at first by a viscid liquid called *protoplasm*, having an abundance of small granules floating in it."—GRAY.

The wall of the cell is composed of carbon, hydrogen and oxygen, and is called *cellulose.* In addition to carbon, hydrogen and oxygen, protoplasm contains a considerable quantity of nitrogen.

Plants grow both in length and size by the multiplication of cells by division, beginning in a single cell in the seed, which, by successive divisions and subdivisions, produces first, the embryo, which, by a continuation of the same process, develops into the plant or tree. New cells can only be formed from the organizable matter already assimilated in the interior of older cells. The enlargement of the stems of exogenous plants is occasioned by the appropriation of organizable matter, which has been prepared in the foliage and passed downward, in consequence of its increased density, by osmose, through successive cells in the inner bark, until it is appropriated to the formation of new cells, either in the production of new rings of cambium, or sap-wood, or of bark tissue.

That stems increase in size by the appropriation of prepared sap from above, is shown by several familiar facts which have fallen under the observation of most farmers.

When a wire is left tightly bound around a stem, it will enlarge more above the wire than below, until, when by continued growth, the stem increases the binding force of the wire, so that enlargement below entirely ceases.

The same phenomenon is seen when a vine entwined about a tree so tightens its grasp as to arrest the descent of the prepared food through the inner bark, an enlargement of the stem takes place *above* the circle of the vine's embrace.

Branching trees increase in size rapidly towards their base, and in proportion to the surface of the foliage exposed by the successive branches. The trunks of palms, which have leaves only at the top, increase in size but little towards the base—not more than may be accounted for by priority of formation.

The same is true, to a great extent, of forest pines, which lose their lower limbs as they increase in height.

The growth of roots is controlled by the same general laws which determine that of stems, as far as the source of *prepared* food is concerned. Their increase in length, as before remarked, is confined to accretion by new cell formation, and never, as in stems, by *elongation*.

Leaves perform an essential function in plant nutrition, as one of the organs of vegetation, since nearly the whole of the organic structure of all plants is primarily received into the organism through them.

Their structure is very complex, their offices manifold, and absolutely necessary for the normal growth and development of the plant.

"In a general, mechanical way, it may be said, leaves are definite protrusions of the green layer of the bark, expanded horizontally into a thin lamina, and stiffened by tough, woody fibres (connected both with the liber, or inner bark, and the wood), which form its framework, ribs or veins. Like the stem, therefore, the leaf is made up of two distinct parts, the cellular and the woody. The cellular portion is the green, pulp, or parenchyma; the woody is the skeleton, or framework, which ramifies among and strengthens the former. The woody or fibrous portion fulfils the same purposes in the leaf as in the stem, not only giving firmness and support to the delicate cellular apparatus, but also serving for the conveyance and distribution of sap.

"The subdivision of these ribs or veins of the leaf, as they are not inappropriately called, continues beyond the limits of unassisted vision, until the bundles, or threads, of woody tissue are reduced to very delicate fibres, ramified throughout the green pulp."

"The cellular portion of the leaf consists of thin-walled cells of parenchyma, containing grains of *chlorophyll*, to which the green color of the foliage is entirely owing."— GRAY.

The upper surface of the leaf seems to be connected with the alburium, or sap-wood, and the lower with the liber, or inner bark.

Assimilation of the food of the plant is carried on in the expanded leaf in the presence of sun-light, which is essential to the perfect discharge of its functions as an organ of vegetation. Under the influence of sun-light, they absorb carbonic acid from the air, which, under the same influence, is decomposed, the oxygen exhaled, and the carbon retained, and combining with the oxygen and hydrogen, forms cellulose.

Besides oxygen, leaves exhale a large quantity of watery vapor into the air, when the condition of the latter is favorable for such exhalation.

"In one of the well known experiments of Hale, a sunflower, three and a half feet high, with a surface of 5,612 square inches exposed to the air, was found to perspire at the rate of twenty to thirty ounces avoirdupoise every twelve hours, or seventeen times more than a man. *

A seedling apple tree with eleven square feet of foliage, lost nine ounces a day." (Gray.)

The leaves of plants, therefore, not only supply the air with pure oxygen, so necessary to animal life, but afford a vast amount of watery vapor when the air is dryest, and most in need of moisture. The meliorating influence of extended forests upon climate may be readily understood, when we consider the vast aggregate of evaporating surface presented by their foliage.

The baleful effects of a promiscuous destruction of the natural forests in the interior of continents, remote from large bodies of water, are probably largely due to the interruption of this beneficial exhalation.

Since all of the water contained in plants, and that exhaled from their leaves, is absorbed by the roots, the importance of an abundant supply of moisture to the latter is apparent. If the evaporation from the leaves is less than the absorption of water by the roots, the plant remains fresh, and if other circumstances are favorable, grows rapidly; if, however, as often happens in periods of continued drouth, the exhalation of watery vapor from the leaves is in excess of the absorption by the roots, the leaves wilt, and the plant suffers.

The same effect is seen when, in summer, the careless plowman breaks the roots of plants, and thus curtails their absorbing surface. Every farmer has seen the ill effects of breaking the roots of corn and cotton in summer. Recognizing this fact, the branches of trees are partially removed at transplanting, to readjust the equilibrium between the stem and the remaining roots.

The *organs of vegetation*, roots, stems and leaves have been briefly described, and their offices explained in general terms.

ORGANS OF REPRODUCTION embrace the flower and seed, by means of which plants are enabled to perpetuate their species.

"The flower," says Gray, "is a branch intended for a peculiar purpose. While a branch with ordinary leaves is intended for growing, and for collecting from the air, and preparing or digesting food, a blossom is a very short and special sort of branch, intended for the production of seed. The parts of the flower, excepting the receptacle, answer to leaves."

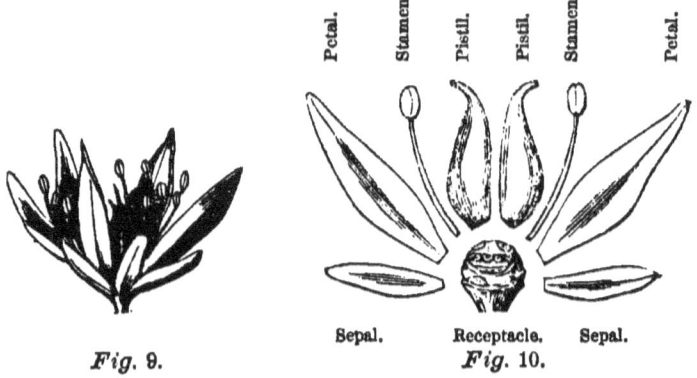

Fig. 9.   Fig. 10.

Fig. 9 represents a flower complete in all its parts. Fig. 10 shows the different parts of the flower in pairs, separated from the end of the flower-stalk (receptacle) but standing in their natural position.

The *stamens* and *pistils* are the immediate organs of reproduction. Fig. 11 represents a complete flower in which both of these organs appear. Fig. 12 an incomplete flower, having stamens but no pistils.

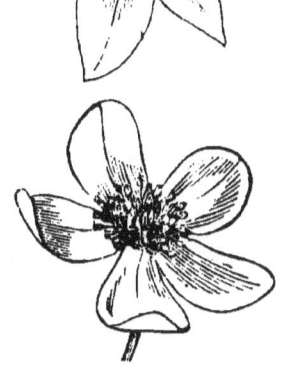

Fig. 11.

Fig. 12.

Some plants have uniformly complete flowers which are independent of the winds and insects for their fertilization. To this class belong the cotton plant and small grain. Others have the pistillate and staminate flowers on separate parts of the plant, and are entirely dependent for fertilization upon winds and insects. To this class belong Indian corn, which has the staminate flower in the tassel, and the pistillate in the silk; and the melon family, which have a large number of staminate flowers attached to long stems, and a few pistillate flowers attached to the young melon which represents the ovary. These are usually fertilized by bees and other insects, which carry the pollen from the staminate to the pistillate flowers and thus facilitate fructification.

Others still have pistillate and staminate flowers on different plants. This is seen in the willow, poplar, persimmon, hemp, some varieties of strawberries, etc. Others still have staminate, pistillate and complete flowers on the same plant.

The *stamen* consists of two parts, the *filament* or slender stem, and the *anther*, which is a hollow sack on the top of the filament filled with a fine yellow powder, called *pol-*

len, which being deposited upon the *stigma* of the pistil fertilizes the ovule or embryo seed at its base.

Pistil Magnified.
Fig. 13.

The *pistil*, represented by Fig. 13, is composed of four principal parts: The *stigma*, which is an enlarged, porous, moist, roughish and naked body (having no skin covering like the other parts) terminating the *style*, which connects it with the *ovary* at the base of the pistil; within the ovary or seed pod, is the *ovule* or embryo seed.

The pollen grains falling from the anther of the stamen on the stigma, or conveyed to it by the winds or insects, in some way not yet fully understood, exerts an influence upon the ovule or embryo seed, which results in the production of seed.

It is not deemed necessary to enumerate in detail, the different forms which flowers assume, the object being simply to convey an idea of the essential parts of flowers, in connection with the process of fructification and reproduction.

To still further illustrate these, Figure 14 represents a vertical section of a cherry blossom, in which are shown the sepals, petals, stamens, pistils, ovary, and ovule. This is a complete flower, but it will be observed that the sepals, petals and stamens, all branch out from the margin of a thickened cup, which is only the base of the *floral envelope* which embraces both calyx and corolla, which are the basis of the flower-vase, one of the principal offices of which is to protect the *essential organs*, the stamens and pistils. The sepals, all taken together, form the calyx; the petals, collectively, form the carolla.

The Circulation of Sap will now be considered only so far as a knowledge of it may be thought useful to the farmer.

All of the functions of vegetable nutrition may be expressed in three words, viz: *imbibition*, assimilation and growth.

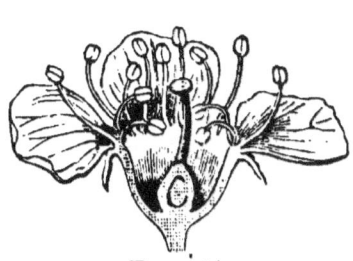

Figure 14.
Section of cherry blossom, showing every part of the flower.

Imbibition takes place through the root-hairs, the leaves and green parts of the bark, principally by osmose, but to some extent by capillary attraction, and is confined to liquids and gases, the former being derived chiefly from the soil, the latter principally from the air. All of the ash element (that which remains when vegetable matter is burned in the air,) of plants is imbibed in solution in water by the roots, as well as some of the organic elements which pass off into the air when the plant is burned. The importance of this root action will be appreciated when it is remembered that plants, in the fresh state, contain from 70 to 90 per cent. of water.

The following tables, taken from Johnson's "How Crops Grow," show the percentages of water in some common agricultural products, *fresh* and *air-dried*. These percentages vary in different plants of the same species, and in the different parts of the same plant. The amount varies also at different stages of growth, with the amount of moisture in the soil in which it grows, and the humidity of the air by which it is surrounded.

WATER IN FRESH PLANTS.	
	Per Cent.
Meadow Grass	72
Red Clover	79
Maize, as used for fodder	81
Cabbage	90
Potato Tubers	75
Sugar Beets	82
Carrots	85
Turnips	91
Pine Wood	40

WATER IN AIR-DRY PLANTS.	
	Per Cent.
Meadow Grass (Hay)	15
Red Clover Hay	1
Pine Wood	20
Straw and Chaff of Wheat, Rye, etc.	1
Bean Straw	18
Wheat, Rye, Oat, (kernel)	14
Maize (kernel)	12

Since no mineral substance can be taken into the plant except in a state of solution, it is not only necessary that there should be an abundance of moisture in the that the mineral elements of plant-food shall be in a soluble condition before they can be made available to the plant. The water in the soil enters the absorbing surfaces of the roots of the plants mainly by osmodic imbibition, certain vegetable acids being expelled by exosmose from the root-hairs, which act chemically upon the mineral substances of the soil, as is plainly shown by the etching of smooth marble by the roots of plants which rest upon it during their growth. Capillary force may also participate in this imbibition, when a rapid evaporation of watery vapor is progressing from the surfaces of the leaves.

This liquid, (soil water,) freighted with *unorganizable* or *crude plant-food*, passes by osmodic action from cell to cell, until millions of these receptacles have been traversed in its passage to the leaf where, spread out under the influence of sunlight, it is assimilated—converted into more condensed *organizable plant-food* by the evaporation of watery vapor, and the exhalation of oxygen.

The contents of the cells of the leaves being thus rendered more condensed, the prepared sap passes downward from cell to cell, is appropriated to the growth of the plant by cell division over the entire growing surface of the plant, thus perpetuating the process so long as the surrounding circumstances of warmth and moisture are favorable.

Leaves imbibe from the air, carbonic acid gas, which is decomposed under the influence of sunlight into its elements, carbon and oxygen, the former retained, and the latter, to a large extent, exhaled into the air again. During the night carbonic acid is exhaled, and oxygen retained.

The *volume* of oxygen exhaled during the day is about equal to that of the carbonic acid imbibed during the same time.

Sunlight is necessary for the healthy development of vegetation, as is shown by the white appearance of potato sprouts which grow in dark cellars.

In cases of drouth the mineral food held in solution by the liquid imbibed by the roots is too highly concentrated, and often produces injurious effects upon vegetation apart from those resulting from drouth proper. This is frequently seen where highly ammoniated commercial fertilizers have been applied in large quantities in the drill, to summer crops.

CHAPTER III.

CHEMICAL COMPOSITION OF PLANTS.

The whole physical world is divided into *organic* and *inorganic* substances.

The first embraces all bodies which have resulted from *life*, and includes both the vegetable and animal kingdoms.

The second embraces all bodies not the result of life, as well as the remains of organic bodies reverted by complete decomposition to mineral form.

All organic substances are composed of volatile and fixed, or ash, ingredients.

The volatile part, which constitutes on an average about 95 per cent. of the whole plant, is composed of carbon, oxygen, hydrogen and nitrogen, with very small quantities of sulphur and phosphorus. They are called volatile elements because they are driven off and mingled with the atmosphere when the organism is burned in the open air.

The ash elements which remain after the burning as solids, are chiefly phosphorus, sulphur, silicon, chlorine, potassium, sodium, calcium, magnesium, iron and manganese, and also small quantities of oxygen, carbon and nitrogen. A few other elements are found in very small quantities—too small to require notice here. The *elements* are given in the above enumeration, but they are usually taken into the organism, and appear in the ash as compounds.

These elements, and their principal compounds of any importance in connection with agriculture, have already been described.

These various substances, volatile and fixed, enter into the same plant in a uniform ratio to each other, but in very different percentages. The *importance* of any constituent, however, bears no relation to the per cent. in which it is found in the plant. In one sense they are all of equal importance, since the plant cannot attain to full development without the presence of all of these elements, which naturally enter into its composition, in the necessary ratio to each other.

Though the ash elements occur in relatively very small quantity, they are essential to the perfect development of the plant, and are, together with nitrogen, the first which need to be artificially supplied to the soil. The atmosphere affords an inexhaustible source of the prominent volatile elements of plant food.

Wolff and Knop give the following percentage from all the trustworthy analyses made of agricultural plants—all of them air-dried, except the last:

	Water.	Organic Matter.	Ash.
Average of all the grasses	14.3	79.9	5.8
Average of grains and seeds	14.2	83.3	2.5
Average of straw	14.4	80.2	5.4
Average of chaff and hulls	13.7	77.7	8.6
Average of roots and tubers	85.7	13.4	1.9
Average of green fodder,	79.5	18.8	1.7

—Scientific Agriculture.— Pendleton.

These analyses show how small is the per cent. of ash ingredients in plants in proportion to the volatile part.

Nearly the whole of the volatile part, except the water and ammonia, is derived from the atmosphere, while the entire ash is derived from the soil.

The following tabular view of the relations of atmospheric ingredients to the life of plants, given by Prof. Johnson in "How Crops Feed," page 98, presents the subject in a condensed form :

TABULAR VIEW OF THE RELATIONS OF THE ATMOSPHERIC INGREDIENTS TO THE LIFE OF PLANTS.

Absorbed by Plants.
- OXYGEN, by roots, flowers, ripening fruit, and by all growing parts.
- CARBONIC ACID, by foliage and green parts, but only in the light.
- AMMONIA, *as carbonate*, by foliage probably at all times.
- WATER, as liquid, through the roots.
- NITROUS ACID, } *united to ammonia*, and dissolved in water through the roots.
- NITRIC ACID,
- OZONE? } Uncertain.
- MARSH GAS?

Not absorbed by plants.
- NITROGEN.
- Water in state of vapor.

Exhaled by Plants.
- OXYGEN, } by foliage and green parts, but only in the light.
- OZONE,
- MARSH GAS, in traces by aquatic plants?
- WATER, *as vapor*, from surface of plants at all times,
- CARBONIC ACID, from the growing parts at all times.

In speaking of the chemical composition of plants, the *ultimate constituents* or *elements* will be seldom mentioned, since they are never taken up by plants in their elementary forms, but as *proximate principles*, or compounds.

To illustrate: Carbon is taken into the plant in the form carbonic acid gas; phosphorus, as phosphoric acid; nitrogen, as ammonia, nitric acid, etc.

The proximate organic principles are divided into "carbohydrates, albuminoids, vegetable acids, vegetable oils, alkaloids, and coloring matters."

Carbo-hydrates, so named from being composed of carbon hydrogen and oxygen, are subdivided into woody fibre, starch, sugar, gums, and jellies, all of which are objects of interest to a greater or less extent to the agriculturist.

Cellulose, the principal constituent of woody fibre, forms a very large part of all vegetable structure, serving as the framework of the organism, and especially of the cell walls.

"Cellulose exists in various vegetable matters, when airdried, in the following proportion:

	Per cent.		Per cent.
Potato tuber	1.1	Clover hay	34.0
Wheat kernel	3.0	Maize cobs	38.0
Maize kernel	3.5	Oat straw	40.0
Barley kernel	8.0	Wheat straw	48.0
Oat straw	10.3	Rye straw	54.0

—Scientific Agriculture.—Pendleton.

Lignin is more dense, contains more carbon, and is less digestible than the cellulose.

Starch is very abundant in many vegetables, and especially so in many seeds and tubers. It is found within the cell-walls in very minute grains. It is made from various grains and tubers, by first grating, grinding, or otherwise pulverizing the substance, so as to break the cell-walls, when the powder or flower is washed with water, the starch grains held in suspension allowed to settle, the water poured off, and the deposited starch dried. Or, the albuminoids may be dissolved out by a weak solution of caustic soda before washing.

Cellulose and *Starch* are identical in chemical composition; each having:
Carbon............44.44
Hydrogen............6.17
Oxygen............49.39

100.00

Dextrine, also identical in chemical composition with celullose and starch, is found in old potato tubers and the unripe wheat plant. It may be made artificially from starch, and is used extensively in the arts, especially in printing calicoes. In baking bread, a portion of the starch is converted into dextrine, the latter sometimes amounting to as much as ten per cent.

The gums constitute an important product from many plants, and are extensively used in commerce. They are convertible into grape sugar by long boiling in water.

Von Bibra gives the following percentage of gum in various substances air-dried:
Wheat kernel............4.50
Wheat flour............6.25
Rye flour............7.25
Barley flour............6.33
Oatmeal............3.50
Rice flour............2.00
Wheat bran............8.85
Rye kernel............4.10
Millet flour............10.60
Corn meal (maize)............3.05
Buckwheat flour............2.85
Spelt flour............2.48

Pendleton.

Sugar occurs in the several forms of cane sugar, fruit sugar, grape sugar and milk sugar.

Cane sugar, saccharose, derived principally from sugar cane, sugar beet and the sap of the sugar maple, that from the sugar cane constituting the great bulk of the sugar of commerce. Pure *cane* sugar, free from water, consists of:

Carbon..............................44.92 per cent or 12 atoms
Hydrogen........ ....6.11 " " " 10 atoms
Oxygen...........................48.97 " " " 10 atoms

The following table will show the average percentage of saccharose in the juice of several plants ("How Crops Grow," p. 13.):

Sugar cane...................18 per cent............Peligot.
Sugar beet...................10 per cent............Peligot.
Sorghum..... .... 9½ per cent.............Goessman.
Indian corn in tassel...... 3½ per cent.............Ludersdoff.
Sugar maple sap.......... 2½ per cent.............Liebig.
Red maple................. 2½ per cent.............Liebig.

Saccharose is twice as sweet by weight as glucose.

Grape sugar or glucose is found in the juices of many plants, in honey, etc. In the malting of grain a portion of the starch is converted into glucose. It is composed of carbon, 40.00, hydrogen 6.6, and oxygen 53.33.

Fruit sugar or fructose, though identical with glucose in chemical composition, is much sweeter, does not crystallize, and is found generally combined with other sugars, in honey, molasses, and fruits.

Milk sugar—Lactose, is found only in the milk of animals, and is prepared from the whey of milk in some countries. Its chemical composition in 100 parts is: carbon, 42.10; hydrogen, 6.40; and oxygen, 47.00.

Von Bibra found saccharose, glucose or fructose in the following percentages in the flour of different grains:

Per Ct.
Wheat flour..2.33
Wheat bran...4.30
Rye flour......... ....3.46

	Per Ct.
Rye bran	1.86
Corn meal	3.71
Barley meal	3.04
Barley bran	1.90
Oat meal	2.19
Rice	0.39
Buckwheat meal	0.91

—(Scientific Agriculture—PENDLETON.

Alcohol is produced from sugar, by fermentation, in the presence of water, at a temperature of from 60° to 90° Far.

It is also produced from plants, seeds and tubers containing starch, the latter being first converted into sugar, and then into alcohol.

Cellulose, starch, sugar, dextrine and gum are mutually convertible in nature, and to a considerable extent in the laboratory. "Thus in germination, the starch of the seed is converted into dextrine and glucose, and in this form passes into the embryo to nourish the plantlet. Here, again, it changes into cellulose and starch. In the sugar beet (which is destitute of starch, but contains 10 to 14 per cent. of sugar), in certain diseased conditions, the sugar is transformed into starch."

The principal vegetable acids are, malic, tartaric, citric, oxalic, tannic, acetic, vinegar and prussic.

Malic acid is found in various fruits, deriving its name from *Malum*, the Latin for apple. It is never found pure in nature.

Tartaric acid is found in the grape, combined with potash, and in the fermentation of wines is deposited as tartrate of potash. From this salt purified, the cream of tartar of commerce is derived. It is used as a medicine, and the acid is an ingredient of Seidlitz powders.

Citric acid is found in the juice of the lemon, lime and other fruits of the citron family. Its compound with iron, citrate of iron, is used in medicine.

Tannic acid is found in the bark and leaf of the oak and other trees and plants. Its principal use is in tanning leather. It is also used with copperas in making ink.

Oxalic acid is found in considerable quantity in the sorrels. It is a powerful acid, having a remarkable affinity for lime, even displacing sulphuric acid. Hence an application of lime is beneficial to the lands of Southern Georgia, on wnich the sorrel grows, its effect being to neutralize this and other injurious vegetable acids. The presence of sorrel in considerable quantity may be regarded as an indication that lime is needed.

Acetic acid is the sour principle of *vinegar*, which is an impure form of acetic acid, resulting principally from the fermentation of the juices of fruits, but is also produced from any liquid containing sugar, by the use of a ferment, by the oxidation of alcohol, from infusion of malte and from a mixture of starch and yeast.

Mother of vinegar, which consists of an aggregation of microscopic plants (ulvina aceti) is produced in acetous fermentation which it not only facilitates, but probably causes.

Vinegar is made rapidly from fermented or fermentable liquids, by passing them repeatedly through oaken barrels filled with beech shavings, previously steeped in strong vinegar, increasing the temperature of the liquid at each filtration. Vinegar made from wine or cider is most highly esteemed for domestic uses.

Prussic acid is found in a very dilute state in the bark and leaves of the cherry, and peach, and also in the kernels of most stone fruits. It is present in considerable quantity in the bark of the wild cherry, the medicinal properties of which are attributed to the influence of this acid.

Vegetable oils are divided by distinct characteristics into fatty or fixed oils, and essential or volatile oils. These exist as minute, transparent globules in the cells of plants, and may generally be extracted by simple pressure. In the common bayberry and the tallow-tree of Nicaragua, however, the fat, being solid at ordinary temperatures, requires heat for its extraction. The principal source of commercial vegetable oils, are the seeds of flax, cotton, hemp, sunflower, colza, pea-nut, butter-nut, the castor-bean, etc., in which the per cent. of oil ranges from 10 to 70. The principal difference between the fatty and the volatile oils as indicated by their names, is found in the non-volatile character of the former, and the volatility of the latter. Fatty oils dropped upon paper leave a grease spot, while the volatile oils entirely evaporate, leaving no trace of grease.

"The proportion of fat in certain vegetable products is given by Wolff and Knop, as follows:

Maize fodder (green)	0.5	Indian corn	7.0
Red clover (green)	0.7	Wheat	1.5
Cabbage	0.4	Rice	0.5
Pea-fodder (dry)	2.0	Oats	6.0
Clover hay	3.2	Peas	2.5
Wheat staw	1.5	Barley	2.5
Average of all the grains	2.6	Winter rye	2.0
Potato (Irish)	0.3	Pumpkin	0.1
Turnips	0.1	Beet	0.1

The Albuminoids or Protein Bodies are classified in three groups. The type of the first is *albumen*, which is found nearly pure in the white of an egg; of the second, *fibrin*, represented by animal muscle; of the third, *casein*, or the curd of milk.

Animal Albuminoids differ very little from the vegetable from which they are primarily derived. In both the living or undecayed vegetable and animal matters they are principally soluble in water, but are very readily rendered insoluble by coagulation.

They differ from the carbo-hydrates in having in addition to carbon, hydrogen and oxygen, 15 to 18 per cent. of nitrogen, some sulphur, and often a 'small amount of phosphorus. Together they constitute in plants the whole volatile part of vegetation, and furnish the fat and flesh producing principles of animal food.

A knowledge of the relative proportion of these two groups of plant constituents is of prime importance to the farmer, since the efficacy of the food of animals depends, in a large measure, upon the proper combination of the fat and flesh forming principles.

This will be more fully discussed under the head of *Plants and their products as food for animals.*

Vegetable Albumen may be obtained by heating nearly to the boiling point the liquid which is decanted from potato starch, as previously directed, collecting the coagulum which forms on the surface, and boiling it successively with alcohol and ether to remove fat and coloring matters. A substance is thus formed resembling very closely the albumen of eggs.

Albumen may be extracted from the flour of wheat, oats, rye, or barley, by similar treatment of water in which it has been agitated for some time.

Vegetable fibrin may be obtained from wheat-flour, by kneading the dough for some time in a vessel of water, the first product being *gluten,* from which the vegetable fibrin may be dissolved out by alcohol, which latter may be removed by evaporation, leaving nearly pure fibrin. It is soluble in hot alcohol, very slightly in cold alcohol, and not at all in water.

Vegetable casein occurs in peas and beans, as well as in the seeds of other leguminous plants, amounting in some to from 17 to 19 per cent. It very closely resembles animal casein as found in milk. It is found in smaller percentages in other seeds and in tubers.

The Chinese make a vegetable cheese, called *Tao-foo,* by boiling peas to a pulp, straining the liquid, coagulating it with gypsum, and then treating the curd thus obtained in the same manner as milk-cheese is treated.

Prof. Johnson gives, in "How Crops Grow," page 102, the

following table, showing the chemical composition of some of the principal animal and vegetable albuminoids, which will convey to the reader a clear idea of the character and value of this group of substances:

COMPOSITION OF ALBUMINOIDS:

	Carbon.	Hydrogen.	Nitrogen	Oxygen.	Sulphur.
Animal Albumen	53.5	7.0	15.5	22.4	1.6
Vegetable Albumen	53.4	7.1	15.6	23.0	0.9
Blood Fibrin	52.6	7.0	17.4	21.8	1.2
Flesh Fibrin	54.1	7.3	16.0	21.5	1.1
Wheat Fibrin	54.3	7.2	16.9	20.6	1.0
Animal Casein	53.6	7.1	15.7	22.6	1.0
Vegetable Casein	50.5	6.8	18.0	24.2	0.5
Gluten-Casein ⎱ Wheat	51.0	6.7	18.1	35.4	0.8
Gliadin* ⎰	52.6	7.0	18.1	21.5	0.8
Mucedin	54.1	6.9	16.6	21.5	0.9

* Gliadin and Mucedin are two albuminoids which exist in crude wheat gluten.

Since animals have, as far as known, no power of producing the albuminoids, which constitute so large a part of their blood and flesh, but derive them entirely from plants, it is important for the farmer to acquaint himself, not only with the chemical eomposition of the cultivated plants, but also with the means of increasing, by cultivation and fertilization, the percentage of these important substances, by stimulating the production of those parts of the plants which are richest in them.

It is important also that he should know the ratio, existing in different plants, between the *carbo-hydrates*, or fat and heat producing principles, and the *albuminoids* or flesh and muscle producers, that he may know what kind of food to use, to accomplish given results in feeding stock, whether the object be the production of fat, the maintenance of a uniform condition of muscular development, or to encourage the development of a well proportioned muscular frame in young animals. These objects are usually best accomplished by a combination of different foods, as will be more fully explained under the head of *Plants and their products as food for animals.*

The following table from Johnson's "How CROPS GROW,"

gives in a condensed form the percentages of albuminoids in the principal agricultural plants.

AVERAGE QUANTITY OF ALBUMINOIDS IN VARIOUS VEGETABLE PRODUCTS:

Indian corn fodder, green	1.2	Bean straw, air dry	10.2
Beet tops, green	1.9	Meadow hay, air dry	8.5
Carrot tops, green	3.5	Red clover hay, air dry	13.4
Meadow grass, green	3.1	White clover hay, air dry	14.9
Red clover, green	3.7	Buck wheat kernel, air dry	7.8
White clover, green	4.0	Barley kernel, air dry	10.0
Turnips, fresh	1.0	Indian corn kernel, air dry	10.7
Carrots, fresh	1.3	Rye kernel, air dry	11.0
Potatoes, fresh	2.0	Oat kernel, air dry	12.0
Corn cobs, air dry	1.4	Wheat kernel, air dry	13.2
Straw of summer grain, air dry	2.6	Pea kernel, air dry	22.4
Straw of winter grain, air dry	3.0	Bean kernel, air dry	24.1
Pea straw, air dry	7.3	Lupine kernel, air dry	34.5

The ash elememts which remain as solids when plants are burned in the open air, also called the *mineral* or *inorganic* part of the vegetable structure, though constituting a very small part of plants, are nevertheless of prime importance to the vegetable economy, and hence to the agriculturist.

The following table shows the principal elementary substances, found in the ash of plants, and the compounds which they form with oxygen, or with each other. With the exception of sulphur, none of these *elements* are found in nature, but they exist in the soil and in plants as compounds with oxygen, or with each other. Since these compounds are not found in the atmosphere, they must be taken into the plant through the roots, and must, therefore, be present in the soil in an available form to secure the normal development of plants.

Other elementary bodies occur in some plants in very small quantities, but have no important relation to the general vegetation of the farm.

TABLE OF ASH ELEMENTS WITH THEIR COMPOUNDS WITH OTHER SUBSTANCES.

Name.	In combination with	Forming.
Chlorine	Metals	Chlorides.
Iodine	Metals	Iodides.
Sulphur	{ Metals	Sulphurets.
	Hydrogen	Sulphuretted Hydrogen.*
	Oxygen	Sulphuric Acid.
Phosphorus	Oxygen	Phosphoric Acid.
Potassium	{ Oxygen	Potash.
	Chlorine	Chloride of Potassium.
Sodium	{ Oxygen	Soda.
	Chlorine	Chloride of Sodium or Common Salt.
Calcium	{ Chlorine	Chloride of Calcium.
	Oxygen	Lime.
Magnesium	Oxygen	Magnesia.
Aluminum	Oxygen	Alumina.
Silicon	Oxygen	Silica.
Iron and Manganese	{ ...Oxygen	Oxides.
	...Sulphur	Sulphurets.

*Called also Hydro-sulphuric Acid.
†Agricultural Chemistry.—*Johnson*.

Since plants can take up no solid matter, however finely divided, all of these substances must be either in a soluble condition in the soil, or readily rendered so by reagents existing in the soil. As their character, and the sources of each, have already been given, their further discussion will be resumed under the heads of PLANT FERTILIZATION, SOIL FERTILIZATION, and FERTILIZERS.

CHAPTER IV.

PLANT FERTILIZATION.

There are two methods of ascertaining what elements of food different plants require:

1st. By the analysis of the plants themselves, the chemist learns what they contain, and in what ratio the different elements enter into their composition.

2d. By experiments in growing plants under circumstances in which all the conditions of growth are known, and in which the effect of different elements of plant-food can be definitely ascertained. Indeed, plant analysis, soil analysis, and experiment, are all employed in conjunction, to ascertain the needs of different plants.

Seeds are planted in soils of known composition, to which different elements of plant-food, in various quantities and ratios, are added, and the results compared.

Science is thus enabled to know, not only what kinds of food are required for different agricultural plants, but the proportions in which they unite in each.

By reference to the Tables in the Appendix, it will be seen that in the ash of most of our cultivated plants, potash and phosphoric acid play a conspicuous part.

Not only do these enter largely into the ash of these plants, but it is a well established fact that they are earlier exhausted from the soil than any other mineral elements, and hence must be supplied artificially by the farmer.

These, together with nitrogen, are the principal constituents necessary to be artificially supplied on most soils, though soda and lime are often applied with satisfactory results.

As shown by the Tables, tobacco is a large consumer of all of the principal elements of mineral plant-food, and is, consequently, the most exhausting crop grown in the South. While the analysis of plants indicates very accurately the kind and per cent. of the constituents which enter into the organism, a knowledge of the character of the soil, and feeding capacity of the plants, is necessary to determine to what extent these constituents should be artificially applied.

In plant fertilization, the farmer aims to supply each crop with just those constituents in kind and quantity which are supposed to be necessary to the production of the maximum crop. These constituents are varied in kind, quantity and ratio, to suit the requirements of different plants, and are also modified by circumstances of soil, temperature and supply of moisture.

To illustrate: the tobacco planter requires a fertilizer richer in potash than in phosphoric acid, with a liberal percentage of ammonia, lime, magnesia, chlorine, and soda, unless these ingredients already exist in abundance in the soil. The cotton planter requires more phosphoric acid than potash, which together, with ammonia, are the principal ingredients of the fertilizers usually applied to cotton.

Plant fertilization is generally practiced in Georgia, and in all other States where land is cheap, and large surfaces cultivated. It is a temporary resort for immediate results; and though securing profitable crops, seldom permanently improves the quality of the soil, unless combined with judicious and systematic rotation of crops, involving both protection from summer suns, and a return to the soil of a large part of the vegetable matter produced. It is the most economical method of fertilization, where immediate returns are sought, since the plant-food is applied in such mechanical and chemical condition, and in such proximity to the roots of the plant, as to be promptly available, and thus returning principal and interest in the first crop, under favorable meteorological conditions both as to temperature and moisture. In plant fertilization the manure is applied in the hill or drill, the method usually employed in Georgia, so that the first roots put forth reach the manure, and thus give the plant an early, vigorous start. This effect has been particularly marked in North Georgia, in pushing forward the cotton plant and hastening its maturity, in advance of early frosts. Indeed, this system of plant fertilization has extended the area of profitable cotton culture about fifty miles north of the original limit, since its effect is to practically lengthen the season of growth about one month, by causing the plant to mature its fruit about a month earlier than that cultivated without manure in the drill. A similar advantage is realized in the original cotton belt, in enabling the planter to gather his crop in better condition, and before the weather grows too cold for expedition in the tedious process of cotton picking. Indeed, before the present system was adopted, more cotton was picked in January than is gathered now in December.

The organic constituents of plants, with the exception of nitrogen, are supplied in sufficient quantity from the atmosphere, which is beyond the control of man. It is now universally agreed by scientists who have investigated the matter, that carbon, which forms so large a part of vegetation, is derived from the air, in combination with oxygen, as carbonic acid, and hence it is not necessary for the farmer to apply carbon to the soil as plant food. There are elements of plant-food, however, which the farmer not only *may*, but in many instances *must*, apply to the soil to secure remunerative crops. The principal of these are nitrogen, phosphoric acid and potash, and on some soils, and for some plants, lime, magnesia and soda; the last three being generally present in sufficient quantity in the soil for most plants. The fact, however, that some of these elements are more important to man, on account of the necessity of their artificial supply, does not imply that one is more important in plant nutrition than another. Each is equally important to the plant to the extent to which it enters into its composition, since the plant cannot be perfectly developed without the proper *combination* of its chemical constituents. In the entire absence of phosphoric acid, perfect seed cannot be formed; without carbon, neither woody fibre, starch, nor sugar can be produced.

The analysis of an entire plant shows the percentage and ratio in which each constituent enters into its composition; and taking into consideration the character of the soil to be planted, the nature and analysis of the plant to be cultivated, and the fact that the so-called organic elements, except nitrogen, are supplied by the air, the farmer may supply the mineral ingredients in quantity and ratio necessary to the production of a given crop.

Prof. Levi Stockbridge, of Massachusetts, has reached some remarkable results by experiment on different crops, in which he predicted beforehand the increased production, as the effect of the fertilizers applied. Some of his results are very remarkable, and show a wonderful triumph of science, as applied to agriculture.

His experiments, conducted for several years, illustrate two important facts, viz.: that potash, nitrogen and phosphoric acid are generally the only elements of plant-food necessary to be added artificially to the soil, for the production of our agricultural plants, (except, perhaps, tobacco, which requires more magnesia than is usually found in soils,) and that by the application of these three elements, in an absolutely soluble condition, in the ratio to each other in which analysis shows them to enter into particular plants, a given number of bushels or pounds of these particular plants may be produced, within certain yet unknown limits, in a measure proportionate to the quantity of the fertilizer applied.

A few out of the number of experiments conducted, either by himself or by others under his direction, with uniformly satisfactory results, will suffice to illustrate the method pursued and the results attained.

Two equal plots at the college farm were planted in corn, and treated alike in every respect, except that one had no manure, while enough potash, phosphoric acid and nitrogen, mixed in the proper proportion, and used in sufficient quantity to make twenty-five bushels of corn, with the natural proportion of stalks, were applied to the other, with a small surplus, which he supposed the roots of the plants would not get the first year. The plot without manure yielded thirty-five bushels, and the manured plot yielded sixty-four and four-tenths bushels, or four and four-tenths bushels more than were required. He sent, the same year, the same quantity of fertilizer to Mr. Hurd, at Hadley, in the same State, stating that it would give an increase of twenty-five bushels over the production of the unaided soil, which was very poor. The unmanured plot produced eighteen bushels, the manured plot forty eight— five more than was predicted. Concluding, therefore, that the surplus application was not necessary, he applied the next year just the quantity thought necessary to give *fifty* bushels more than the production of the soil without manure. The result was that the unmanured plot produced thirty-four bushels to the acre, while the manured plot gave 83.28 bushels to the acre.

Similar experiments were conducted with potatoes, oats, hay and beans, with correspondingly satisfactory results. Not only so ; but the same plots planted the second year, gave a large increase over the unmanured plots; showing that the effects of the manure continued through the second year. These experiments have not been conducted sufficiently long to establish the principle, but the results thus far justify further experiment on the same line.

While plant fertilization alone generally gives satisfactory results, its effects are much more satisfactory when used in connection with soil fertilization, especially when green manuring is resorted to as a means of soil improvement.

CHAPTER V.

SOIL FERTILIZATION.

This, though embracing plant fertilization, and having for its ultimate object the supply of food for plants, differs from it in several material respects.

One is special, direct and partial, and designed to affect a particular crop, while the other is general, indirect, and designed to permanently improve the soil, and supply nourishment to more than one generation of plants. One supplies just those elements of plant-food in ratio to each other, and in aggregate quantity sufficient to nourish particular plants; the other supplies all the elements of plant-food to *the soil as a reservoir* from which any plant may select the particular elements necessary for its nutrition.

One is temporary and looks to immediate returns—the other is more permanent, improving the capital invested in land, and increasing the returns through a series of years.

As population becomes dense, and a higher rate of production is rendered necessary for its support, as well as to insure a reasonable per cent. upon the enhanced value of lands, soil fertilization is combined with plant fertilization to insure both prompt and continuous returns.

THE MEANS USED.

To secure the permanent improvement of a soil, it must not only be abundantly supplied with the various elements of plant-food in forms either available or readily rendered so, but the mechanical condition must be such as to afford the free expansion of the roots of plants, and to freely absorb, and retentively hold, moisture and ammonia.

It is, therefore, necessary to supply three classes of substances to the soil to compass these ends, viz : *actual plant-food*, *chemical agents*, and *mechanical agents*.

Actual plant-food, or *fertilizers proper*, embrace all the mineral elements of plant-food, and one volatile—nitrogen.

Phosphoric acid and potash are the only mineral ingredients which are so far exhausted as to require artificial application to most soils, though soda, lime, magnesia, and, for some plants, chlorine in small quantities are sometimes added. Lime, which acts in the triple capacity of fertilizer, chemical agent, and mechanical agent, is present in most soils in sufficient quantity to meet all demands for it in the first capacity.

Phosphate rock and animal bones furnish the chief commercial source of phosphoric acid.

Potash, next in importance to phosphoric acid, is exported from Germany in the two forms of sulphate of potash and chloride of potassium.

From hard wood ashes it is obtained as carbonate. It is furnished also to soils, by the decomposition of igneous rocks containing felspar. In some instances the debris of these rocks is, in some localities, deposited in vast beds in connection with marl, known as green sand marl. There is a deposit of this marl in Houston, and other counties both east and west of it, which analyzes from two to three per cent. of potash.

Farm-yard manure, which is a complete manure in the sense of containing all of the elements of plant-food, has in all time been used in soil fertilization, and answers an admirable purpose when applied broadcast in large quantities; but the supply is too limited, especially in a planting region, to accomplish the purpose on a large scale.

The chief reliance for soil improvement on a large scale must ever be the growth of leguminous plants, to be returned to the soil, in connection with the application of the principal mineral elements in conjunction with a judicious rotation of crops, which require the mineral elements in different proportions.

The plants used in this country for this purpose are clover, the field pea or bean, and common vetch.

Dr. St. Julien Ravenel, of Charleston, South Carolina, has been conducting some very interesting experiments on the coast lands of his State, in which he applies what he calls the ash element, composed of 500 pounds of calcined marl, and 1,000 pounds of ground phosphate rock and 500 of kainit, to peas on cultivated lands, and to vetch on meadows, at the rate of 400 or 500 pounds per acre.

The growth of the peas and vetch is materially increased on the coast lands of South Carolina, by the application of the so-called ash element, and the vines being either plowed into the soil, or left to decay on its surface, restore whatever of plant-food they have derived from either artificial or natural sources to the soil in available forms to be used by succeeding vegetation.

The following extract from the report of a special committee of the Agricultural Society of South Carolina, shows some of the effects of this system on the coast lands of that State, the only artificial application being 500 pounds of the so-called ash element.

EXTRACT FROM REPORT OF COMMITTEE OF SOUTH CAROLINA AGRICULTRAL SOCIETY, MADE MARCH 22, 1878.

"The report of Mr. Albert M. Rhett, of the Atlantic Phosphate Works, to this Society, in November last, on experiments with these fertilizers under the direction of Dr. St. Julien Ravenel, is relied upon for this fact. Mr. Rhett told us in his paper of 45 bushels of Indian corn, of 50 bushels of oats on land previously so poor that, without manure, it would not make above five of corn and eight of oats; of wheat grown at the rate of 40 bushels per acre, and of 9,000 pounds of hay to the acre produced through these vetches and this ash element." The hay was made from Bermuda grass.

The mineral matters are fed to the legumes, peas and vetch, which decay and supply these and the nitrogen they contain, to the succeeding crop. The results of this system, so far, have been very remarkable on the coast lands of South Carolina, and give promise of important influences upon the agriculture of the *coast regions* of the Carolinas' and Georgia.

CHEMICAL AGENTS.

Lime is the principal *chemical agent* which is artificially applied to soils.

Its chemical action in the soil is varied and important. Its first, and most important, effect is in neutralizing acids in the soil. by forming chemical combinations with them, and in this way is said to *sweeten* the soil.

This effect is particularly noticeable when it is applied to soils containing injurious acids, resulting from the decomposition of vegetable matter in the presence of an excess of water. With some of these acids it unites, forming insoluble compounds, but with most of them, soluble compounds are formed, from which plants derive important nutritive constituents.

A deficiency of lime is indicated by the presence of certain acid plants, such as the sorrels, for instance, which contain oxalic acid, which is poisonous to the most of our cultivated plants.

Lime combines with this acid, forming oxalate of lime, a compound which is insoluble in water, but exists in a dissolved condition in the cells of growing plants.

The prevalence of the sorrel in the southern part of Georgia plainly indicates the absence of lime in those soils in sufficient quantity to neutralize the poisonous effects of the oxalic, and other injurious acids which they contain, and that its application would prove beneficial.

Lime also decomposes mineral compounds, preventing the injurious effects of some, while it liberates others, and places them at the disposal of the plants.

The decomposition of organic matter is hastened by the presence of lime in the soil, and compounds important to vegetation are formed with the result of such decomposition. Vegetable acids thus formed are neutralized by the lime, and nitrogen contained in the organic matter is rapidly liberated and converted into ammonia, nitrate of lime, or nitric acid—forms from which plants appropriate this necessary element.

Since lime is dissolved by water charged with carbonic acid, the presence of decomposing vegetable matter, one of the results of which is the evolution of this gas, facilitates the decomposition of the lime, renders it soluble, and hence increases its distribution in the soil.

Caustic lime, however, is freely soluble in water, and is not only readily distributed through the soil, but rapidly carried down beyond the reach of vegetation.

Since quick-lime is soon converted into the carbonate in the soil, its *chemical* effect differs but little from that of chalk or marl, but, being more finely divided, is more active and available.

Lime, besides acting directly as plant-food, and chemically in the preparation of other substances, exerts also an important influence as a mechanical agent.

Sulphuric acid, carbonic acid, ammonia, and potash, also act both as direct plant food, and as chemical agents.

The interest of farmers demands the most economical means for both plant and soil fertilization, which should, as far as practicable, be combined. For this purpose, the pea-vine and lime in some form, together with compost of cotton seed, animal manures and superphosphate, furnish at present the most promising sources for the farmers of Georgia. Marl is locally accessible in a large portion of Southern Georgia, and quick-lime in all of Northwest Georgia, and, indeed, may be readily transported to almost any part of the State at reasonable rates, as soon as it is used in sufficient quantity to justify its being quarried and burned on a large scale.

COMPOSTS.

Georgia produces annually about 17,500,000 bushels, or 525,000,000 pounds of cotton seed. About 2,000,000 bushels are required for planting the crop, leaving 15,500,000 bushels—232,500 *tons* of seed to be used for manurial purposes. If the whole of this was composted with animal manure and superphosphate, according to the formulæ published in the circulars of this Department, there would be produced 620,000 tons of compost; enough to manure, at the rate of 300 pounds per acre, 4,133,333 acres, or at the rate of 500 pounds per acrè, 2,480,000 acres.

The area planted in corn, wheat, oats, rye, barley, rice, cotton, tobacco, sugar cane, sorghum, sweet potatoes, Irish potatoes, ground peas, and vineyards, in Georgia, according to the returns of the tax receivers, in 1875, was 4,494,724 acres.

By carefully husbanding home manures of every kind, and composting them with superphosphate containing a small per cént. of potash, derived from kainit, or chloride of potassium, enough manure may be composted on Georgia farms, by a comparatively small outlay for potash and phosphoric acid, to manure on the plan of plant fertilization, nearly the whole cultivated crops of the State.

This, if used in conjunction with pea vines turned under in the fall, and lime and marl spread broadcast over the land for soil fertilization, would very rapidly renovate the worn lands of the State.

For formulæ for composting, see Appendix.

MECHANICAL AGENTS.

Lime, marl and vegetable matter are the principal mechanical agents, and should invariably be used together, since each materially increases the efficacy of the other.

Lime acts mechanically upon stiff soils by loosening them, rendering them more friable, and hence facilitates the penetration of the roots of plants. It also stiffens light soils by pulverizing the coarse particles, and thus rendering them more compact.

Vegetable matter turned into the soils, either green or dry, has the following effects when reduced to the condition of humus

1. Humus renders stiff soils friable and open.

2. It absorbs moisture from the atmosphere, and thus supplies plants with it.

3. It retains the moisture longer than any other ingredient of soils.

4. It furnishes a considerable portion of carbon to plants either directly or indirectly.

5. In its widest sense, it supplies the mineral elements of decayed matter in soluble forms for plant-food.

6. It absorbs and holds free ammonia and its carbonate, and thus supplies plants.

7. It absorbs lime and its carbonate, and renders it assimilable as plant-food.

8. It furnishes a solvent to the soil (carbonic acid), for the silicate of potash and phosphate of lime, by which plants are supplied with the two important compounds, phosphoric acid and potash.

9. In warm climates, it cools the soil by the alternate imbibition and evaporation of moisture.

10. It is, in fact, a prime agent in the laboratory of nature, for carrying on chemical changes in soils, producing heat, evolving carbon, oxygen, and hydrogen, as well as nitrogen, obtained by absorption.—[Scientific Agriculture.—Pendleton.]

One of the causes of the remarkable effects of composts upon the denuded soils of Georgia, may be attributed to the humus which they contain.

A word of caution in relation to the use of lime, may prevent disastrous results to the inexperienced. *Lime should not be applied to soils deficient in vegetable matter*, without a simultaneous application of either coarse manure or vegetable matter of some kind.

It should not, however, be mixed with animal manures, or any other containing any considerable percentage of nitrogen, before it is spread upon the soil. It converts nitrogen into ammonia, which is volatile, and will pass off as a gas into the atmosphere.

This action of liberating ammonia is beneficial if it takes effect in the soil, where it is immediately absorbed and retained, by humus or clay, for the use of plants.

These cautions apply only to quick-lime, or the carbonate; sulphate of lime has the opposite effect of *fixing* the ammonia in an available form—the sulphate—and hence its incorporation with animal manures is very desirable.

From forty to fifty per cent. of pure, high-grade super-phosphate is sulphate of lime, or gypsum, and hence the application of gypsum to composts, in which superphosphate is used, is not necessary.

The beneficial effect of sulphate of lime, when applied as a top-dressing to plants, especially to legumes, is attributed to its power of fixing ammonia from the air.

THE ATMOSPHERE IN ITS RELATIONS TO VEGETATION.

There is a mutual relation between the atmosphere, plants, and animals, which beautifully illustrates the econiomy of nature.

The atmosphere is a mechanical mixture of oxygen and nitrogen, with small quantities of carbonic acid, ammonia, and watery vapor. Its composition is nearly invariable at all points on the surface of the earth, its uniformity being preserved by winds and currents.

Though the per cent. of carbonic acid in the atmosphere is extremely small, plants derive all of their carbon from it, through the medium of their leaves and other green parts.

"Every six pounds of carbon in existing plants have withdrawn twenty-two pounds of carbonic acid gas from the atmosphere, and replaced it with sixteen pounds of oxygen gas, occupying the same bulk."—GRAY.

The carbo-hydrates, or heat and fat producing constituents of plants, sometimes called the ternary compounds, from the fact that they are composed of three elements—carbon, hydrogen, and oxygen—are derived principally from the atmosphere; though the hydrogen is probably absorbed entirely by the roots, in water, and oxygen in part from the same source.

While the composition of the atmosphere cannot be changed by man, it is supposed that the application of sulphate of lime (gypsum) to the surface of plants facilitates the absorption of a portion of its nitrogen as ammonia.

Rain, also, especially when accompanied by electricity, carries down to the soil, for the use of plants, ammonia from the atmosphere.

In periods of drouth, the evaporation of moisture from the surface of the leaves of plants is often in excess of its absorption by their roots, and wilting of the leaves and general contraction of the plant results. The plants resume their normal condition during the night, by the restoration of the equilibrium between the evaporation from the leaves, and the absorption of moisture by the roots.

Unlike the soil, the atmosphere cannot be exhausted either of its constituents necessary in plant nutrition, or of the oxygen essential to animal respiration.

When we consider the vast amount of carbon in the vegetation which covers our globe, and that the whole of it has been derived from the atmosphere, the question naturally arises, "How is this carbon restored to the air?" The carbon in all vegetation is derived from the atmosphere in the form of carbonic acid.

This is a product of the decay and combustion of vegetation and animal matters, the combustion of coal and oils, and of the respiration of animals.

Each decaying leaf, each flickering taper, each respiration of an animal, however small, yields up its contribution of carbonic acid to the atmosphere.

Plants absorb carbonic acid during the day, through their leaves and other green parts, assimilate the carbon, and give off the oxygen to the air, while a small quantity of carbonic acid is given off during the night. Animals retain the oxygen, and exhale carbonic acid at all times, thus illustrating the beautiful harmony and economy of natural laws.

Carbonic acid is essential to the life and growth of plants, oxygen to the respiration and life of animals. They reciprocally supply each other's wants. Plant life is, however, independent of animal, since all of the carbonic acid contained in vegetation consumed by animals, would, in the natural process of decay, be returned to the air without the intervention of animals, which only expedite its return ; but animal existence is absolutely dependent upon vegetation.

Animals consume, either directly or indirectly, only what plants produce. They produce but little directly from the mineral world.

Graminivorous animals feed upon vegetation only, to supply food for carnivora, so that it is almost literally true that "all flesh is grass."

There is another reciprocal relation between the atmosphere and vegetation, which is of great practical importance, and which man may to some extent control.

This is found in the mutual influence of vegetation and the moisture of the atmosphere upon each other.

Plants, by evaporation from their leaves, restore a vast amount of moisture to the atmosphere, and thus materially meliorate its condition.

"A recent experimant made by Knop, showed that a dwarf bean exhalted, in 23 days in September and October, 13 times its weight of water. He further established the fact, that a grass plant will exhale its own weight of water in 24 hours in the hot, dry days of summer; and that a maize plant exhaled 36 times its own weight of water from May 2d, to September 4th."—[Scientific Agriculture.—PENDLETON.]

From these facts, some idea may be formed of the vast amount of moisture which is exhaled in the aggregate, by the whole vegetation of the globe. It demonstrates also the folly of a wholesale destruction of forests. It is a well known fact that the destruction of forests causes the gradual drying of the climate.

CHAPTER VI.

SOILS IN THEIR RELATION TO VEGETATION.

Soils naturally depend for their mineral elements upon the source from which they are themselves derived, but their fertility often depends more upon artificial treatment than original source.

All soils owe their origin primarily to rocks, and are ameliorated by vegetation, the larger part of the latter having been derived from the atmosphere.

Soils, as regards their origin, are classed as *sedentary* and *transported*.

Sedentary soils are those which overlie the rocks from which they have been formed. A very correct idea of their original mineral constituents may be obtained from those of the underlying rocks, allowing of course for modifications resulting from the process of decomposition, and subsequent treatment. Such soils are found in Middle and North Georgia.

Transported soils are such as have been drifted from the locality of the parent rocks, and deposited by the agency of glaciers or floods, in regions less elevated than those in which they originated.

Transported soils are subdivided into *drift, alluvial* and *colluvial*, according to the circumstances of their deposition.

Drift, is found on the border of the primary and tertiary formations of this State, extending from Augusta across to Columbus, and may be distinguished by the presence of rounded, water-worn pebbles and boulders, imbedded in the soil.

It is supposed to have been deposited at the close of the Glacial Period.

Alluvial soils result from the deposits of material transported by running waters, which hold them in suspension until their course is sufficiently interrupted to cause the deposit of the suspended material, as sediment. Successive deposits, continued through a long period, form stratified alluvial soils.

Colluvial soils are mixtures of drift and alluvial, containing both rounded and fractured rocks.

Agriculturally, soils are classified as *sandy, clayey, calcareous* or *marly*, according to their composition. Soils containing a large per cent. of vegetable matter, or humus, are called *vegetable moulds*.

Those in which sand predominates, but is united with a considerable amount of clay, are termed *sandy loams;* where the proportions of sand and clay are reversed, they are termed *clay loams*.

It is important that the farmer should understand, not only the physical character, but the chemical constituents of the soil he cultivates.

There are very few soils of such physical and chemical character as to be permanently independent of the use of artificial means, either to perpetuate their fertility, or to restore the waste from successive cropping.

The physical condition of soils may be affected by a variety of artificial means, at the command of the landlord.

Soils composed of coarse sand allow a too rapid descent of water through them; are incapable of supplying moisture from below, by capillary attraction, and are deficient in the power of absorbing moisture or fertilizing gases from the atmosphere. Neither are they retentive of fertilizers applied to them. Where a clay subsoil underlies them, in reach of the plow, their mechanical defects may be somewhat remedied by bringing up the clay, during winter, to be mingled by the action of frosts and rains, with the surface sand.

The clay fills the interstices between the grains of sand, increases its retentive and absorptive power for moisture and gases, improves its capillary action, and facilitates root action. The addition of vegetable matter in conjunction with the admixture of clay, will more effectually correct its mechanical defects.

If clay is not in reach of the plow, the use of lime with vegetable matter is the most economical and effectual means to be employed to ameliorate the defective mechanical condition of coarse sandy soils, and thus increase their productive capacity.

Clay soils are called *heavy* on account of the difficulty attending their cultivation, though their specific gravity is less than that of sandy soils, which are called light, on account of the facility with which they are cultivated.

The stiffness and tenacity of clay soils is remedied by an application of lime and vegetable matter, which serve as divisors, preventing the adhesion of the particles under the influence of either drouth or excessive wet.

Clay soils are often injured by being plowed when too wet, especially in the spring, when drying winds, and a baking sun, cause a harshness, which continues throughout the growing season, and often, in our mild climate, lasting through several years.

Though more difficult to cultivate than sandy soils, clay has a much greater capacity for absorbing and retaining moisture and fertilizing gases from the atmosphere.

Clays deficient in vegetable matter, or without an admixture of sand, often contract, when dry, to such an extent as to break the rootlets of plants, and thus cause serious injury. This does not occur in sandy soils or loams.

Dry, pulverized clay may be advantageously used as an absorbent in stables, to fix fertilizing gases, and especially ammonia, which would otherwise escape into the atmosphere, and be, to a large extent, lost. A notable illustration of its absorbing power, and consequently deodorizing power, is found in its use in the commode, or "earth closet."

Tainted meats may be sweetened by being buried for a time in clay soil.

Color and texture of soils exert a very decided influence upon the absorption and radiation of heat, both of which depend materially upon their absorptive and retentive powers for moisture.

It has been found, by experiment, that the difference between soils whitened and blackened was nearly the same as that between the same soils wet and dry. It has been further shown that the difference due to color is confined principally to the *surface*. Schubler sprinkled lamp-black and magnesia on the surfaces of different dry soils, and tested the temperatures which they attained. He found that the blackened soils attained a temperature of from $13°$ to $14°$ higher than the same soils whitened; and that the range of increase varied not more than $2.5°$ in the different soils.

He also compared various soils in their wet and dry states, and found the *increase* of temperature in the dry, over the wet soils, corresponded very nearly with that due to the dark color, but that the whitened dry soil became warmer than the natural color wet, and that the blackened dry soils exceeded in temperature those of the natural color about as much as the blackened did the whitened.

Soils which have stagnant water sufficiently near the surface to be reached by the roots of ordinary cultivated plants, are usually cold and unproductive. Thorough underdraining of such soils not only affords relief from the stagnant water, but permits the surplus from heavy rains to pass off readily, facilitates cultivation, permits a free circulation of atmospheric air, pregnant with its burden of watery vapor and fertilizing gases, and elevates the temperature of the soil, enabling vegetation to start forth with full vigor in early spring.

It is difficult to estimate the importance of such a pulverization of the soil as to admit of a *free circulation of air*. Every observant farmer has noticed the difference in the amount of moisture which accumulates by deposition from the atmosphere, during a single summer's night, on soil freshly stirred, and on that covered with a crust which excludes the air. Some idea of the amount of moisture thus extracted from the air may be formed from the accumulation of dew upon vegetation. The more finely a soil is pulverized, the greater the surface presented to participate in robbing the atmosphere of its moisture, for the benefit of vegetation. Again, deep preparation and thorough pulverization of the soil enables it to store up moisture, which is yielded up to vegetation during drouth, by capillary attraction. Soils thus prepared absorb and retain water from heavy rains, which would run off to the streams from those poorly prepared, carrying with it a portion of the surface soil. Proper preparation, therefore, converts a destructive into a productive agent.

MINERAL PLANT-FOOD IN THE SOIL.

This is a question of special importance to the advanced agriculturist, since by availing himself of the light which science has thrown upon plant nutrition, he can not only ascertain what elements of plant-food his soil contains, but may supply its deficiencies in the character, quality, condition and ratio needed by different agricultural plants.

Chemical analysis shows, approximately, the chemical composition of the soil, and quite accurately that of plants. Knowing, therefore, not only the elements of mineral food required by each plant, but the ratio in which they enter, the farmer may supply; for each crop, the mineral elements that are found to be deficient in the soil, either naturally, or as the result of partial exhaustion, by successive cropping, washing and leaching.

The principal mineral elements obtained from the ash of plants, are sulphur, phosphorus, silicon, chlorine, potassium, sodium, calcium, magnesium, iron and manganese. Oxygen and carbon are also found in small quantities. These, together with nitrogen and hydrogen, constitute all the important elementary substances found in agricultural vegetation.

But few of these substances are utilized by plants in their elementary forms, oxygen being probably the only one. Sulphur is taken up by plants as sulphuric acid, silicon as silica, chlorine in the form of chlorides, potassium as potassa or potash, sodium as soda, calcium as lime, magnesium as magnesia, iron and manganese as oxides of these metals, carbon as carbonic acid, nitrogen as ammonia and nitric acid, oxygen in its free state and in various combinations, hydrogen in water and ammonia. This is not intended as an exhaustive enumeration of the forms in which these substances are taken up by plants, but only to show that, with the exception of free oxygen, they are appropriated from their various *compounds*, instead of from their *elements*.

These ash elements are essential to the full development of plants; the total absence of any one of them being fatal to their very existence. In this sense, therefore, they are of equal importance to vegetation.

In another sense, however, some have much greater importance to the agriculturist than others. It is unnecessary to consider those elements, which are derived from the atmosphere, since its composition is practically beyond man's control. It is with the soil that the farmer must deal, and on his knowledge and skill in treating this, his success will depend. The term Agriculture, means the cultivation of the soil, but its *cultivation* does not embrace the full scope of the farmer's duty, though an important part of it.

He must not only acquaint himself with the physical peculiarities of his soil, and learn to remedy its defects, but he must ascertain, either by analysis or experiment, or by both conjointly, the *chemical* constituents of his soil, in order that he may know to what crops it is best adapted, and what elements of plant-food need to be artificially supplied.

With a knowledge of the physical and chemical requirements of the different cnltivated crops, and a familiarity with the physical character and chemical composition of the soil, the farmer may, by supplying the deficiences of the latter, fulfill the requirements of the former.

Phosphoric acid and potash are the first mineral ingredients exhausted from cultivated soils, and generally the only ones which need artificial application. These, with nitrogen, form the valuable part of most commercial fertilizers. Many soils are naturally deficient in lime, and it is often leached through the surface on others, rendering its application not only desirable but necessary. Soda and magnesia are beneficial, as special manures, to particular plants.

Plants differ materially in the kind and quantity of mineral matter required for their production, and thus are exhaustive of the soil in different degrees. The following analysis of tobacco, cotton fibre, cotton seed, and wheat showing the amount of different mineral matters contained in 1,000 parts of each, will illustrate this fact:

	Volatile Matter.	Ash.	Potash.	Soda.	Magnesia.	Lime.	Phosphoric Acid.	Sulphuric Acid.	Silica.	Chlorine.
Tobacco	760	240	65.76	8.88	25.20	68.80	8.64	9.36	13.04	10.80
Cotton fibre	987	18	4.22	1.06	1.14	3.02	1.30	0.62	0.18	0.90
Wheat	980	20	6.25	0.70	2.44	0.62	9.24	0.48	0.34	Not estimated.
Cotton seed	963	37	11.24	1.44	5.01	8.84	12.17	1.39	0.39	0.61

An inspection of the foregoing analyses develops important facts, which the farmer may use to his advantage.

Ist. They show the principal mineral elements required by each plant for the production of those parts which are removed from the soil, and which, if not already present in the soil, must be supplied by the farmer.

2nd. They show the different degrees to which these plants exhaust the mineral elements of the soil, if only the marketable products are removed. Thus, if the cotton seed and stalks are returned to the soil, only the lint being removed, and the whole tobacco plant be removed, 1,000 pounds of the latter will extract from the soil $15\frac{1}{2}$ times as much potash as 1,000 pounds of the former, 8 times as much soda, 22 times as much magnesia, more than 29 times as much lime, 6 times as much phosphoric acid, 15 times as much sulphuric acid, 72 times as much silica, and 12 times as much chlorine. This explains the rapid exhaustion of lands by the removal of successive crops of tobacco, without compensative returns of manure. Comparisons similar to the above may be made by the reader from the Tables of the Appendix.

3rd. They indicate to the farmer the elements which should be combined, both in kind and relative quantity, for the production of particular plants. The advantage of such knowledge is forcibly illustrated by the remarkable results of the experiments of Prof. Stockbridge on plant fertilization, which have already been cited.

It should be remembered, however, that most soils, not absolutely barren, are store-houses of mineral substances which, under the influence of natural agencies, are constantly undergoing mechanical and chemical changes, which gradually convert inert substances into available, assimilable forms. In these transformations, the alkalies, carbonic and sulphuric acids, and vegetation, both dead and living, perform an active part.

A soil may be rich in all the mineral elements of plant-food, but if they are not in a soluble condition, or readily rendered so, they are absolutely worthless to plants. Natural agencies, however, are constantly at work, both mechanically and chemically, upon the mineral compounds of the soil, pulverizing them, forming new compounds, or destroying those already formed.

"Water, charged with carbonic acid and oxygen, is constantly circulating up and down through the soil, acting upon the silica, lime, phosphoric acid and potash, rendering then soluble, and supplying them directly to the feeders of the plants."

"Air is indispensable to the soil, to prepare food for plants, by the chemical action of oxygen and carbonic acid."—Sc. Agr.

In order to secure a free circulation of air in the soil, thorough drainage and deep tillage are necessary.

"The advantages of drainage are not confined to land which is absolutely *wet*, but its beneficial effects will be experienced in all those soils in which water can remain stagnant, at any time, at a less depth than three or four feet beneath the surface. Like shallow tillage, want of drainage compels the roots of plants to remain near the surface of the ground, where they are not only exposed to all the vicissitudes of weather, but are also compelled to seek their nourishment within very narrow limits. Drainage, therefore, loosens and aerates the soil and subsoil, in such a manner that the roots of plants are enabled to penetrate deeper, to strata which are rarely, or never, sufficiently affected by drouth, to allow injury to vegetation."
—(Hilgard—Agl. Rept. Miss.)

To sum up, the effects of drainage are:

The soil is made porous and productive, by being warmer, and by having a greater depth for the roots.

The lands dry faster after a rain, and yet resist drouth better.

Fertilizers act better.

It prevents washing away of the soil, and, consequently, of fertilizers.

It prevents miasma and malaria by carrying off stagnant water.

It not only improves the mechanical condition of the soil, but facilitates chemical action, which results in the decomposition of vegetable matter, and the increased solubility of mineral compounds.

, It prevents the formation of acid compounds, poisonous to vegetation.

It facilitates the preparation and cultivation of the soil, and largely increases its productive capacity.

Subsoiling and deep plowing accomplish some of these ends, but act better in conjunction with under-draining.

Each landowner, however, must determine for himself whether his soil is of such a character as to be sufficiently benefitted by drainage and subsoiling to justify such an investment of time, labor, and capital. The natural drainage of many of our soils is sufficient for agricultural purposes, and no land without a compact (generally clayey) subsoil will be materially benefitted by sub-soiling. Its propriety will depend also upon the chemical composition of both soil and subsoil. This may, to some extent, be determined by *chemical analysis*, of which Prof. Hilgard, in the Agricultural Report of Mississippi, says :

"Analysis teaches us what are the kinds and respective quantities of the ingredients contained in crops, soils, and manures. It teaches us, therefore, which of the latter two will be best calculated to promote the successful culture of the former; to obtain which knowledge by mere experimenting, would require a disproportionate amount of time and labor. The absence of a single one of the ingredients necessary for the growth of a plant renders unavailing the presence of all the rest. Unless we are taught by analysis which ingredient or ingredients, of which there is a deficiency, we shall be compelled, in order to be safe, to add all of them, at great and unnecessary expense; for it will be of no practical advantage to have added an additional supply of those of which there is no lack.

"The importance of reliable analysis of crops, soils and manures is, therefore, obvious enough; yet the mere presence of any useful ingredient in a soil or manure, as demonstrated by analysis, does not yet assure us that it is present in an available condition, so as to be ready for absorption by the plant ; for the agents which the chemist uses in his laboratory are much more powerful than those placed at the command of vegetables by nature ; thus far then, mere ultimate analysis is not a direct indication of the producing powers of the soil.

"This consideration becomes of most serious moment, where the rocks from which the soils are originally derived are in close proximity, so that a large amount of undecomposed material may be supposed to be *unevenly* diffused throughout the soil."

In South Georgia, where the soils have been brought a long distance, and have become more thoroughly intermingled and comminuted, an analysis of a sample, properly selected, would probably indicate very nearly the composition of the soil of a large area.

The aualysis of crops is important in connection with that of soils and manures.

"The determination of the kind and quantity of the mineral ingredients which crops withdraw from the soil is at least equally important with that of the soils themselves. It informs us *what*, and *how much*, the soil has lost in cultivation, and thus enables us to select judiciously the most economical mode of replacing the drain ; provided, of course, that the composition of the fertilizers at our command be also known to us."—*Ibid*.

Soil exhaustion is the result of the withdrawal of the ash ingredients of the crops removed, or of denudation by surface washing.

Complete exhaustion never occurs—the term, as used, being relative only. Complete exhaustion would imply the entire removal of the mineral elements of plant-food from the soil. This is not the sense in which the term is here used. A soil is said to be exhausted when it ceases to produce remunerative crops. This may result from the removal of a single necessary mineral element, the absence of which renders unavailable the others, though present in abundance. Fortunately for man, howeve:, nearly all of the mineral elements exist in practically inexhaustible supply, so that even on the most worn soils, only a few of these elements need be artificially supplied, and these are readily accessible.

Phosphoric acid is, as regards the necessity of artificial supply, first in importance, potash second, and lime, per haps, third; other elements being required in very small quantities for general vegetation.

Generally phosphoric acid and potash, of the inorganic or mineral elements, and nitrogen, of the organic, are all that need be supplied by the farmer to secure remunera tive crops, even from worn soils, if a judicious system of rotation of crops, involving a liberal return of vegetable matter from legumes, to the soil, is practiced.

If all the vegetation annually produced upon the land was returned to it, the soil would annually increase in fertility. If, however, as is usual, a part of the crop is annually removed, mineral substances equivalent to those contained in the portion of the crops carried off must be returned to the land to maintain its normal fertility.

The roots of all plants, and *especially those of the legumes*, have a power of acting chemically upon the mineral compounds of the soil in such manner as to render a portion of them available as plant-food. To this power, in part, is attributed the beneficial effects of the cultivation of the legumes, peas, clover, etc.

The following list shows the amount of mineral ingredients withdrawn from the soil by different crops. It is taken from Prof. Pendleton's "Scientific Agriculture," and is worthy of careful study by farmers:

A crop of 750 pounds of seed cotton will carry off from an acre of land 23.25 pounds of nitrogen, and 33.3 pounds of ash, of which there will be of the most important mineral elements:

Potash............8.30 pounds. Magnesia......5.05 pounds. Sulphuric acid....0.50 pounds.
Soda.........3.20 pounds. Chlorine........0.30 pounds. Phosphoric acid..7.20 pounds.
Lime............6.83 pounds.

A crop of 8½ bushels of wheat, with an equal quantity, by weight, of straw, will carry off 11.50 pounds of nitrogen, and of the mineral elements:

Potash............2.12 pounds. Magnesia........0.74 pounds. Phosphoric acid..2.57 pounds.
Soda..............0.31 pounds. Chlorine........trace
Lime..............0.46 pounds. Sulph'ric acid.0.26 pounds. Total ash........35.15 pounds.

A crop of Indian corn, in the ear, equal to 9 bushels of grain, will carry off from an acre of land, in pounds: nitrogen, 9.00.

Potash..................2.13 Magnesia..................0.76 Chlorine..........trace.
Soda....................0.09 Phosphoric acid..........2.27
Lime....................0.18 Sulphuric acid...........0.09 Total ash..........7.94 pounds.

A crop of oats, grain and straw, allowing that the weight of the straw is double that of the grain, the crop being 12 bushels per acre, will carry off:

Nitrogen........12.0 pounds. Lime............1.62 pounds. Phosphoric acid... 2.27 pounds.
Magnesia.......12.0 pounds. Soda............1.52 pounds. Sulphuric acid..... 0.59 pounds.
Chlorine........trace.   Potash..........4.72 pounds. Total ash..........32.76 pounds.

A crop of peas, consisting of the seed, equal to 9 bushels per acre, will carry off: nitrogen, 16.50 pounds. Mineral substances:

Soda...............0.18 pounds. Sulphuric acid.0.17 pounds. Chlorine........1.11 pounds.
Phosph'ric acid.1.81 pounds. Potash............2.02 pounds.
Magnesia..........0.40 pounds. Lime............0.21 pounds. Total ash......14.05 pounds.

By reference to these tables, the farmer can not only learn the amount of plant-food extracted from the soil by any of the crops mentioned, but has a reliable indication of the amount of those elements, which are first exhausted, that he must apply to the soil to produce a given crop. It is fair to presume that most soils will be benefitted by the application of ammonia, phosphoric acid, and potash, though some probably have a sufficient quantity of each in their virgin state.

Knowing the amount of each element of plant-food required for the production of a given crop, the farmer may calculate beforehand, with a moderate degree of certainty, the increase that will result from the application of a specific amount of plant-food, in the proper combination, if other circumstances are favorable.

To illustrate : If the natural soil will produce 12 bushels of oats per acre, with the necessary amount of straw—assuming that the soil (as is usually the case) contains a sufcient supply of lime, soda, magnesia, sulphuric acid, and chlorine—it may be reasonably expected that the application of 12 pounds of nitrogen, 4.72 pounds of potash, and 2.27 pounds of phosphoric acid, would produce 24 bushels, with the necessary straw, or 12 bushels more than the natural soil ; but the results depend upon such a variety of circumstances, that many experiments will be required to establish the correctness of the assumption.

Since all of the mineral food derived from the soil must pass into the plant in solution in water, each element, to be available to the plant, must be either soluble, or promptly rendered so, by natural agencies, during the period of active growth of the plant.

The influence of climate must be considered in the treatment of soils. This is too often neglected by farmers in the South, whose agricultural literature is principally adapted to more northern climates, where most of such literature has originated.

While the general principles of agricultural science are the same everywhere, their *application to practice* varies according to a multiplicity of circumstances, the influence of which, each individual must decide for himself, according to his surroundings.

Soils in a warm climate are more rapidly exhausted under tillage than those of cold climates, for the following reasons:

1. Vegetation has a longer period of growth in warm climates, in which to extract plant-food from the soil.

2. There is a less rapid and thorough decomposition of

mineral substances by the expanding effects of frozen water, while more of such substances are annually extracted from the soil.

3. The vegetable matter in the soil is more rapidly decomposed under the influence of warmth and moisture, though more needed in warm than in cold climates.

4. Fertilizing gases are liberated more freely in warm climates. This continues throughout the year, where the earth is never covered with snow. Nitrogen, especially, is rapidly removed from the soils of warm climates.

Humus is of more importance, though less abundant, in the soils of warm than in those of cold climates. It serves the double purpose of absorbing and retaining moisture, and thereby cooling the soil, and consequently, is of great benefit independently of the plant-food, which it yields to the soil by its decomposition.

Our climate necessitates different treatment of soils, both in the preparation and cultivation, from that practiced further north.

Winter fallow is less beneficial where the freezes are light, root cutting is more injurious, and level culture, except on bottom land, a necessity.

CHAPTER VII.

FERTILIZERS.

Fertilizers are classed according to their source as *animal*, *mineral* and *vegetable*. These are also called *mechanical*, if their principal influence is exerted in affecting the physical condition of the soil; and *chemical*, if they produce changes in the soil, or furnish plant-food directly to vegetation. There is a distinction made also between *natural* and *artificial* fertilizers.

A fertilizer proper is a substance, either simple or compound, which, when applied to the soil, supplies available plant food in such form as to be readily absorbed by the roots of plants under natural circumstances.

Fertilizing agents aid plants in appropriating plant-food already in the soil without directly supplying it—warmth and moisture are fertilizing agents.

The great bulk of the food of plants is derived from the atmosphere, which is invariable in composition, and beyond the control of human agencies.

It is of such fertilizing substances as may be made tributary to plants through their application to the soil, the productive capacity of which is, to a large degree, under the control of the skillful agriculturist, that this chapter will treat.

The principal fertilizers of animal origin are fish, excrementitious matters from animals and fowls, and the flesh, blood, bones, horns, hoofs and hair of animals.

Fish and fish scraps, the refuse from oil factories, are used as a commercial source of ammonia, of which it contains over five per cent., with a moderate per cent. of phosphoric acid. It is used for the purpose of supplying ammonia to commercial compounds.

The fish, however, decomposes so promptly that its nitrogen is, in a very short time, converted into actual ammonia, which, being all promptly available, acts injuriously in cases of drouth, and is exhausted before the period of growth of our summer crops is completed. For the cotton plant, which continues its growth throughout our long summers, a part should be actual, and a part potential ammonia, or nitrogen, in such a form as to be capable of being converted into ammonia. In the case of fish, the decomposition is so rapid that its entire nitrogen is promptly converted into actual ammonia, and hence the tendency of fertilizers, ammoniated with fish, to "fire" crops in times of drouth.

Excrement varies in its composition:

1. That of no two varieties of animals is alike in chemical composition.
2. That from the same animal varies with the character of the food consumed.
3. That from young growing animals is less valuable, especially in phosphoric acid, than that from grown animals.
4. That from fat animals is richer in nitrogen than that from those in a lean condition, where much of the food consumed is appropriated to the restoration of flesh as well as fat.
5. That from fowls is richer than that of animals, because the solid and liquid excrements are combined.
6. Liquid excrement of all animals is richer in plant-food than the solid, and should, as far as practicable, be saved by farmers.

Flesh, blood, horns, hoofs and hair are rich in nitrogen, and are used by manufacturers of commercial fertilizers to supply that important element to their compounds. The percentage of nitrogen contained in them ranges from six to sixteen. Dried flesh and blood are very extensively used as sources of ammonia, by manufacturers of fertilizers. The dried flesh is derived principally from countries where animals are killed in large numbers for their hides, horns and tallow, and the flesh boiled for extract of meat. "The fibrinous residue, when dried, becomes a most advantageous nitrogenous material for use in the manufacture of ammoniated fertilizers."

Dried blood is derived from the extensive slaughter-houses of the United States, and other countries, where millions of animals are slaughtered for food. The blood is either dried, or solidified by coagulation, and thus is formed a condensed mass, exceedingly rich in nitrogen. Dried ox-blood contains from fifteen to seventeen per cent. of nitrogen.

Mineral fertilizers are those substances which, derived

primarily from minerals, are found in the ash of plants, when they are burned with free access to the air. The most important are potash, soda, lime, magnesia, phosphoric acid, sulphuric acid, silica, and chlorine. Of these, phosphoric acid may be said to be always beneficial, as an artificial application to the soil, potash generally, lime often, soda, chlorine, and magnesia, for particular plants, such as tobacco, beets, etc., and the others, never.

Phosphoric acid is derived principally from animal bone, phosphate rock, as found near Charleston, S. C., and in various other parts of the globe, and from the decay of animal and vegetable matters. Its principal office in plant nutrition, seems to be to increase the production of fruit, and especially seed, rather than stalk. By reference to the Tables of Analyses, in the Appendix of this work, the reader will see that it is an important constituent of the ash of the seeds of all agricultural plants.

Soda is derived, principally, from the *chloride of sodium*, or common salt, which abounds in the waters of the ocean, in salt springs, and in vast deposits of rock salt. It is present in sufficient quantity, in most soils, for the purposes of vegetaiton, but may be profitably supplied, as a special fertilizer, to a few plants, such as tobacco, beets, turnips, carrots, etc.

Salt (*chloride of sodium*) is especially beneficial to cabbage and asparagus, and applied to gardens, in early winter, is destructive of injurious insects.

Nitrate of soda is found as an incrustation on the surface of the earth, in Peru. It acts finely, when applied as a topdressing, on small grain and the grasses.

Potash is used for agricultural purposes, in the various compounds of potassium, which, uniting with carbonic acid, forms carbonate of potash; with sulphuric acid, sulphate of potash; with chlorine, chloride of potassium, (muriate of potash); with nitric acid, nitrate of potash, nitre, or saltpeter, and with silicic acid, silicate of potash.

The latter is formed naturally in soils, by the disintegration of rocks containing feldspar or mica. The granites of Georgia yield this form by decomposition.

Carbonate of potash is found in wood ashes, which furnishes a cheap, but limited source, of this important and necessary constituent of all fertile soils. The caustic property of lye is due to potash leached from the ashes. Leached ashes differ from unleached only in the per cent. of potash contained—both are valuable as fertilizers.

Sulphate of potash is derived, principally, from *kainit*, which is extensively mined near Strassfurt, Prussia. Kainit contains from 23 to 25 per cent. of sulphate of potassa, from 14 to 28 per cent. of magnesia salts, and 30 to 48 per cent. of chloride of sodium. Pure sulphate of potassa contains 54 per cent. of potassa, and 46 per cent. of sulphuric acid. Kainit is the best commercial source of potash, for the reasons that the foreign matters associated with it are, to some extent, valuable as an application to the soil, the sulphuric acid acting as a chemical agent for the reduction of other substances in the soil, the magnesia salts and chloride of sodium serving as plant-food, and the alkalies being presented in such combinations as not to volatilize ammonia from nitrogenous substances, with which the farmer or manufacturer may desire to compound it.

Chloride of potassium is another important source of potash. It is derived mainly from the mines near Strassfurt, Prussia, where it is found in a vast bed of clay, overlying one of rock salt. When pure, it contains 52.35 per cent. of potassium and 47.65 of chlorine.

Nitrate of potash, commercially known as nitre or saltpeter, is procured from certain districts in India, and from caves, by simply leaching the earth with water, and evaporating the solution thus obtained. It is also made from artificial nitre beds, in many parts of Europe.

Lime exists in nature in vast quantities.

1st. As carbonate of lime, which is composed of lime

and carbonic acid. It is found abundantly in nature in the shells of marine animals, in coral, chalk, marble and limestone. These shells and rocks, "when strongly heated, especially in a current of air, part with their carbonic acid, and quick-lime remains behind."

Carbonate of lime is found in considerable quantity in the ashes of most plants, and especially in those of trees. Quick-lime, or caustic lime, when taken from the kiln, is a hard, dry substance which, when exposed to the air, slowly absorbs moisture, becomes air-slaked, and crumbles to a fine powder, in which form it is readily applied to, and easily mingled with, the soil. Quick-lime is a compound of calcium and oxygen.

Air-slaked lime is extensively applied to cultivated lands in Europe, and portions of the United States. It acts beneficially upon stiff, clay soils, by rendering them open, and hence more readily penetrable by rain, air and the roots of plants. It facilitates decomposition of vegetable matter and coarse manures, and, by chemical action upon insoluble minerals in the soil, renders them available as food for plants. It also, to some extent, furnishes food directly to the roots of plants. By its action upon vegetable matter, in breaking down its organic structure, it not only liberates the mineral substances which the organic matter contains, but converts the potential into actual ammonia.

It should not be applied to soils denuded of vegetable matter. An important effect of lime in soils is found in the neutralization, by its alkaline property, of injurious vegetable acids.

Since lime has a tendency to sink into the soil, it should be applied to the surface. The quantity to be applied, and the frequency of the application, will depend upon the character of the soil and its previous treatment. In some countries large quantities are applied at long intervals, while in others smaller applications are made, at shorter intervals.

In portions of England, as much as 250 to 300 bushels of slaked lime are sometimes applied per acre, followed by applications of from 8 to 20 bushels every four or six years, according to circumstances. Larger applications may be made to stiff clays than to sandy soils, and in either case the quantity should depend somewhat upon the depth of the soil, and the amount of vegetable matter it contains. Again, since vegetable matter decomposes more rapidly in warm than in cold climates, larger applications are generally admissible to soils in the latter than in the former.

Lime should be invariably applied broadcast, and thoroughly incorporated with the soil, if applied without previously composting with vegetable matter.

Lime should never be composted with animal manures, or other substances containing a considerable percentage of nitrogen. If composted with such material, the loss of ammonia will result.

To secure the full benefit of liming, the soil, if not naturally so, should be first thoroughly under-drained.

If marls are used, the quantity applied per acre should depend upon the per cent. of carbonate of lime they contain, and upon the physical character of the marl used, as regards its pulverulent condition or the facility with which it crumbles before or soon after its application to the soil.

The necessity of an application of lime to any particular soil, may be determined to some extent, by the character of the spontaneous growth, but more accurately by experiment on a small and comparatively inexpensive scale.

Another, and very important form in which lime occurs in nature, is in combination with sulphuric acid, known to the chemist as *sulphate of lime*, and to commerce as gypsum, ground plaster and land plaster.

It contains lime............. ....32.56 per cent.
Sulphuric acid.. ....46.51 " "
Water............................ .... 20.93 " "
                                              ———
                                              100.00 " "

It is found in extensive beds in different parts of the world, and after being ground to a powder, is much used in old agricultural States as a top dressing for small grain and pastures.

It constitutes from 40 to 50 per cent. of every commercial superphosphate, in which it occurs as a surplus ingredient, resulting from the treatment of the phosphate of lime with sulphuric acid, and costs the consumer nothing.

If, therefore, superphosphates are used, there is little necessity for applying gypsum.

Its beneficial effects have been attributed by some to the sulphur of the sulphuric acid, by others, to the action of the sulphuric acid in fixing ammonia from the atmosphere, and by others still, to the lime, while each probably contributes somewhat to the benefit derived from its use. Its action on plants, especially on the legumes, is often very remarkable, but the particular manner in which it acts is not well understood.

Magnesia is beneficial to some plants and may be deficient in some soils, but is generally present in sufficient quantity to supply the needs of our cultivated plants.

Since kainit is generally employed as a source of potash in commercial fertilizers, a sufficient amount of magnesia is usually incidentally supplied.

Vegetable fertilizers vary in value with the character of the plants used.

They constitute the main reliance for the restoration of exhausted lands, and, indeed, may be regarded as an indispensable factor in this process.

They not only restore to the soil, in readily available forms, the mineral elements and nitrogen derived from the soil, but return, also, vast quantities of those substances taken from the atmosphere to ameliorate the mechanical condition of the soil, and serve as absorbents of moisture and fertilizing gases from the air.

A certain class of plants, known as legumes, embracing the clovers, lucern, peas, beans, and other pod-bearing plants, are especially beneficial as soil fertilizers.

Their long tap-roots penetrate deep into the subsoil, from which they assimilate mineral food, which, after being used in building up the leaves and stems of the plants, is deposited, at their death, on the surface soil, to be used by future crops. Besides this power of deep penetration, this class of plants has greater capacity for decomposing and appropriating mineral matter and nitrogen from the soil than other plants, and are supposed to have a peculiar power of absorbing ammonia from the atmosphere. By reference to the tables of analyses of plants, in the appendix of this work, it will be seen that the legumes are especially rich in nitrogen and the important mineral elements, potash, phosphoric acid, lime, etc. The large quantity of nitrogen which they contain, facilitates their decay, and thus hastens the restoration of their mineral elements to the soil.

The peculiar benefits derived from decayed vegetable matter, have already been given in detail in this work.

By the application of mineral fertilizers to the leguminous plants, their growth is largely increased, and thus their fertilizing capacity improved.

It is a fact well known to practical farmers, that even when the crop of clover or pea vines is removed from the land, its producing capacity for the grasses or cereals is materially increased.

The improvement is still greater when the crop is turned under, or allowed to decay upon the land.

Where there are beds of muck, rich in vegetable matter, it may be banked, in position, during dry spells in summer, mixed with lime, and allowed to remain until convenient to haul out; but if it has to be hauled more than a few hundred yards. the cost will amount to prohibition. *Pea vines and lime furnish not only the cheapest, but the best means, at the command of Georgia farmers as a basis for the restoration of their worn lands.*

Cotton seed, a waste product peculiar to Southern agriculture, afford a most valuable vegetable fertilizer. Georgia produces annually 262,500 tons, and the cotton States 2,-362,500 tons of these seed.

Commercial fertilizers, so extensively used, of late, in Georgia, supply the immediate demand for *plant fertilizers* but furnishing, as they do, principally mineral plant-food in concentrated form, apart from their immediate influence on plant nutrition, they act only chemically upon the soil, which is unable to respond profitably to their application if denuded of vegetable matter.

The improvement in the preparation and quality of the compounds offered to the farmers of Georgia, within the last five years, has been very marked, while their cost has been considerably reduced.

Under the operation of the present inspection laws, as administered, none but reliable compounds can be offered on the Georgia market, and farmers are enabled by the published analyses, largely distributed, to inform themselves as to the chemical composition of every brand admitted to sale in the State.

The principal elements of plant-food in the commercial fertilizers on our market are nitrogen, phosphoric acid and potash. The manufacturers of commercial fertilizers have practically adopted the conclusions of scientific experimenters, that these three elements are *generally* the only ones necessary in artificial fertilizers.

Many, however, misled by the results of experiments conducted on soils in Georgia derived from granite, have omitted potash in the preparation of their compounds, though intended as "complete fertilizers." Others, in response to a demand for superphosphate for composting with stable manure and cotton seed, have omitted both potash and ammonia, assuming that these latter substances would be sufficiently supplied by material already on the farm.

Much depends upon the source from which manufacturers derive the "three elements" of their compounds, as well as upon the forms in which they exist when offered for sale.

The price of nitrogen is estimated, according to its source, at from 25 cents down to 15 cents per pound, phosphoric acid from 12.5 to 3.5 cents, and potash from 9 to 6 cents per pound.

Nitrogen is the most costly element which enters into the so-called complete manures.

The expense of purchasing this, may, to a large extent, be avoided if all of the home manurial resources are husbanded.

By a liberal use of pea-vines as a soil fertilizer, and by supplementing the cotton seed and animal manures of the farm with superphosphate containing a small per cent. of potash, lands may be either improved in fertility, or their normal condition maintained with but little expenditure for nitrogen.

The principal products removed from the farm in Georgia, and sent to market, carry off very little plant-food.

If, therefore, all refuse products are either returned directly to the soil, or fed to animals whose manure, solid and liquid, is applied to the soil, it will require many years, if surface washing is prevented, to become exhausted, even if no artificial fertilizers are used. The true system to be pursued by Georgia farmers is to turn under a crop of pea-vines (or allow them to decay upon the ground) every three or four years; compost with superphosphate, having a small per cent. of potash, all the animal manures and surplus cotton seed of the farm, using these as far as they will go, and supplying the deficiency by the purchase of ammoniated superphosphate.

As the pea vine is the cheapest and best means of *soil* fertilization, so the compost of home manures with superphosphate, is the cheapest and best *plant* fertilizer for our climate and soil. The decomposition of vegetable matter is more rapid in warm than cold climates, and the system of cultivation more destructive of humus. It is, therefore, especially important that due attention be given to supplying this important agent, either in green manures, or in combination with mineral manures of commerce as compost.

The full benefit of commercial fertilizers cannot be reasonably expected in our climate, on soils deficient in humus.

Our farmers have been led into much error, both in cultivation and fertilization by following the teachings of experiments, conducted under circumstances, both of climate, soil, and agricultural practice and products, widely different from those by which we are surrounded.

CHAPTER VIII.

PLANTS AND THEIR PRODUCTS AS FOOD FOR ANIMALS.

The products of the farm may be arranged in four classes:

1. The direct vegetable products, such as the cereals, hay, textiles, roots, etc., which are sold, or used on the farm, in their primitive form.

2. Secondary vegetable products, such as syrups, sugar, etc., which require manufacture before marketing.

3. Such as are the result of a kind of natural manufacture, by which the direct products of the soil are converted into beef, mutton, pork, or wool.

4. Tertiary products, which are a result of artificial con-

version of the secondary products of the natural manufacture of the third class, such as butter, cheese, etc.

"Man, and all domestic animals, may be supported, may even be fattened, upon vegetable food alone. Vegetables, therefore, must contain all the substances which are necessary to build up the several parts of animal bodies, and to supply the waste attendant upon the performance of the necessary functions of animal life."—Elements of Ag'l Ch. and Geol'y.—Johnston.

Indeed the composition of animal substances may be inferred from that of mixed vegetation, since animals that live upon such food, must build up their frames entirely from that source, by simple digestion and assimilation. Vegetation must not only supply the carbon of the fat, the fibrin of the muscles, the saline matters of the blood, and the gelatine of the skin, hair, horns, hoofs, and bones, but must furnish the earthy matters of the bones of animals.

"It is a wise, and beautiful provision of nature, therefore, that plants are so organized as to refuse to grow in a soil from which they cannot obtain an adequate supply of soluble inorganic food—since that saline matter, which ministers first to their own wants, is afterwards surrendered by them to the animals they are destined to feed.

"Thus the dead earth and the living animal are but parts of the same system—links in the same endless chain of natural existences. The plant is the connecting bond by which they are tied together on the one hand—the decaying animal matter, which returns to the soil, connects them on the other."—Ag'l Ch. and Geol'y—Johnston.

There are two classes of substances in plants known to chemists as *albuminoids* and *carbo-hydrates*, the former embracing the flesh-forming principles of the food of animals; the latter the fat and heat producing principles.

The ratio of these substances should vary according to

the kind of animal to be fed, and the object had in view in feeding.

Table showing the proximate composition of Agricultural Plants and Products, giving the average quantities of Albuminoids and Carbo-hydrates in 100 pounds, with their ratio to each other, compiled from tables in *How Crops Grow*:

SUBSTANCES.	Albuminoids.	Carbo-hydrates.	Ratio of Albuminoids to Carbo-hydrates as
Wheat	13.0	67.6	1 to 5.2
Indian Corn	10.0	63.0	1 to 6.3
Oats	12.0	60.9	1 to 5.0
Rice	7.5	76.5	1 to 10.2
Rye	11.0	69.2	1 to 6.3
Millet	14.5	62.1	1 to 4.3
Peas*	22.4	52.3	1 to 2.3
Beans*	25.5	45.5	1 to 1.8
Wheat Straw	2.0	30.2	1 to 15.0
Rye Straw	1.5	27.0	1 to 18.0
Barley Straw	2.0	29.8	1 to 15.0
Oat Straw	2.5	38.2	1 to 15.0
Pea Vines	6.5	35.2	1 to 5.4
Bean Vines	10.2	83.5	1 to 8.3
Corn Stalks	3.0	39.0	1 to 13.0
Pea Hulls	8.1	36.6	1 to 4.5
Potato (Irish)	2.0	21.0	1 to 10.0
Beets (common)	1.1	9.1	1 to 8.3
Rutabagas	1.6	9.3	1 to 5.8
Turnips (white)	.8	5.9	1 to 7.4
Wheat Bran	14.0	50.0	1 to 3.5
Wheat Flour	11.8	74.1	1 to 6.2
Wheat Chaff	4.5	33.2	1 to 7.4
Linseed Cake	28.3	41.8	1 to 1.4
HAY.			
Lucern, in blossom	14.4	22.5	1 to 1.5
Red Clover, in blossom	13.4	29.0	1 to 2.2
Vetches, in blossom	14.2	35.3	1 to 2.4
Orchard Grass, in blossom	11.6	40.7	1 to 3.5
Tall Meadow Oat Grass, in blossom	11.1	35.3	1 to 3
Blue Grass, in blossom	8.9	39.1	1 to 4.4
Timothy, in blossom	9.7	48.8	1 to 5
Average of all the Grasses, in blos'm	9.5	41.7	1 to 4.3
GREEN FODDER.			
Grass, before blossom	3.0	12.9	1 to 4.3
Grass, after blossom	2.5	15.0	1 to 6
Red Clover, before blossom	3.3	7.7	1 to 2.3
Red Clover, in full blossom	3.7	8.6	1 to 2.3
White Clover, in full blossom	3.5	8.0	1 to 2.3
Lucern, very young	4.5	7.8	1 to 1.7
Lucern, in blossom	4.5	7.0	1 to 1.5
Vetches, in blossom	3.1	7.6	1 to 2.4
Oats, in early blossom	2.3	8.8	1 to 3.8
Rye	3.3	14.9	1 to 4.5
Corn Forage } Average of two analyses of corn cut at different stages,	1.0	9.8	1 to 9.8
Peas, in blossom	3.2	8.2	1 to 2.6

*Peas here refer to peas proper, and not to our so-called field pea, which is *really a bean*. The analysis of beans represents approximately that of our "cow pea."

From the albuminoids of their food, animals derive the flesh and muscle of their bodies; from the carbo-hydrates, they derive heat and fat; from the mineral elements of their food, the saline matters of the blood, and the phosphate of lime of their bones are derived.

As in plants, a suitable combination of all these elements which contribute to animal nutrition, is necessary to produce a normal development. The *ratio* in which the constituents of food must exist, depends upon climate, the age and condition of the animals fed, and the purposes for which they are fed.

Nature supplies, in character and variety, the food best suited for man and beasts, in the different zones of the earth. In the frigid zone, an excess of carbon is needed to supply the loss of animal heat consequent upon very low temperature. This is supplied to man in the oils and fat of the lower animals in that region, which accumulate vast quantities of these substances in their bodies. The circumstances of climate demand a liberal consumption of carbo-hydrates to supply the rapid combustion necessary to the preservation of animal heat; and forbid the exertion which, in more temperate climates, causes a waste of muscular tissue.

In the torrid zone, on the contrary, the minimum quantity of the carbo-hydrates is required, since but little carbon is needed to keep up the normal animal heat, while only a small consumption of albuminoids is necessary to supply the waste of muscular tissue incident to the climate. Instead of oils and fats, the denizens of the torrid zone subsist largely upon cooling food, such as fruits and vegetables, which abound in profusion throughout the year.

In temperate zones, where we find the greatest physical and mental activity, nature also supplies food in the necessary variety, and of the proper kind to meet the wants of both man and beast. Here we find the vegetable products of the most solid and nutritious character, having an equitable combination of flesh-forming, fat-producing, and blood and bone-supplying constituents, such as the cereals, grasses and legumes, by a judicious combination of which food adapted to all animals, of whatever age and condition, can be secured.

Again, animals require food containing a larger proportion of carbo-hydrates in winter than in summer. By examining the foregoing tables, it will be seen that hay and the grains, which are consumed in winter, contain a higher per cent. of the carbo-hydrates than the green food which is consumed during summer.

After elaborate experiments in feeding domestic animals, conducted in Germany, it was decided that the best ratio for general purposes, between the albuminoids and carbohydrates is as 1 to 3.

While this ratio exists in only a few single substances, it may be secured by a proper mixture of substances having these proximate principles in different ratios. The practice of many of our farmers who feed corn and fodder throughout the year, regardless of the temperature, is unwise. Corn probably has no superior as winter food for stock, but is too heating for an exclusive summer diet.

Oats make a better summer food than corn, since its flesh-forming principles bear a larger proportion to its fat and heat-producing principles than they do in corn. The green grasses, however, furnish the natural food for animals in summer. Mixed grasses supply the albuminoids and carbo-hydrates in better ratio than single ones, especially when the legumes are mixed with the grasses.

Animals, unconfined, never feed upon a single article, but upon the mixed herbage, which, varying in the proportions of fat and flesh-forming princples, furnish them the means of supplying all their wants. An animal turned into a field in which clover, peas, and corn are growing, will not confine itself to either, but partake of all.

Man does not confine his diet to farinacious nor carbonacious substances, such as fine bread, potatoes, sugar, fats, etc., but mingles with them lean meats and vegetables, to secure a proper combination of fat and flesh producers.

The athlete, while preparing for feats of strength and activity, subsists mainly upon food rich in albuminoids, in order to develop, as much as possible, muscular tissue. The judicious stock-breeder will acquaint himself with the composition of the different kinds of food at his command, and select such as, either alone or by combination with others, will supply his animals with such food constituents as will produce the desired results.

The food will vary with the objects in view. If the object of the breeder is to produce fat, then the food should contain carbo-hydrates in large proportions. If very poor animals, in which the muscular tissue has been wasted, are to be fed, the ratio between the albuminoids and carbo-hydrates should be as 1 to 3, until a normal condition of flesh is restored, when the ratio of carbo-hydrates may be increased. If the production of milk is the object, the normal ratio of 1 to 3, or, perhaps, 1 to 4, in winter, will give satisfactory results. If young growing animals are fed, the normal ratio of 1 to 3, with a liberal per centage of phosphate, for the production of bone, will be desirable.

Animals derive all of their food, either directly or indirectly, from vegetation.

Vegetation is supported from the soil and the atmosphere. All the albuminoids, and most of the carbo-hydrates, came originally from the atmosphere, but are supported largely *through the medium* of the soil. Animals consume plants, and are in turn consumed by them. Plants derive their albuminoid compounds from decayed animal or vegetable matter. Plants take carbon from the air, and return oxygen to it. Animals take oxygen and return carbon. So plants and animals bear a reciprocal relation to each other.

CHAPTER IX.

AGRICULTURAL EXPERIMENTS.

In discussing this subject, the first question to be considered is, what is an agricultural experiment? All of the operations of nature, whether in the vegetable, animal or mineral kingdoms, are controlled by fixed laws, usually called natural laws, or the laws of nature.

The object of science is to ascertain what these laws are, and their relations to each other, or, in other words, to learn from nature, by the interpretation of these laws, the will and mode of thought of the Creator, as expressed in the physical world. Natural science, therefore, bears the same relation to the physical world, that theology does to the spiritual. One interprets God's will, expressed in His creations; the other, his will as unfolded in revelation.

Agricultural experiments have for their object, therefore, the interpretation of God's will in relation to plant life and plant nutrition.

Definitely stated then, an agricultural experiment may be defined as a question asked nature in such form and under such surrounding circumstances, natural or artificial, as to render possible a correct interpretation of the answer from the results expressed in vegetable growth.

The usual object of agricultural experiments is the *de termination of truth* for the benefit of those practically engaged in agriculture.

The first requisite for success is, that the experimenter shall have a clear and definite idea of the question to be asked.

Without this, it is not probable that the proper precautions will be taken to procure the necessary surroundings to secure accurate results, such as are susceptible of correct interpretation.

If the question is clearly understood, and the accompanying circumstances accurately observed, the most difficult task still remains to be performed, viz: The correct interpretation of the answer contained in the results.

Again, surrounding circumstances are often beyond the control of the experimenter, and may vary so as to render the interpretation of the results difficult: hence arises the necessity for frequent repetitions of the same experiment to establish a single truth.

There are two classes of agricultural experiments, differing in the surrounding circumstances.

They may be properly designated as laboratory experiments, and field experiments.

Laboratory experiments embrace those surrounded by artificial circumstances, such as those conducted in pots containing either water or charred sand, to which are added various fertilizing substances, either singly or in different combinations, for the purpose of determining the requirements of plant nutrition. These experiments, every factor of which is known and under the control of the experimenter, are valuable, both in a scientific and practical point of view, since their results are readily interpreted; but the most fruitful of practical results are

FIELD EXPERIMENTS,

which, having natural surroundings, are more valuable to the practical farmer, since they may be locally employed to ascertain the needs of particular soils and plants.

Laboratory experiments are competent to determine general principles of universal application, and thus serve as a valuable guide to the conduct of field experiments.

They ascertain definitely what conditions and substances are necessary for plant nutrition; they add to our knowledge of the general conditions of plant-life, and supply the information necessary as a basis for the conduct of field experiments. They establish general principles; field experiments determine local and definite facts.

The range of field experiment is a very wide one, and

at the same time, in one sense, a very narrow one. It is wide in the range of subjects of investigation, but narrow in its application ; it is wide in the range of useful results to be achieved by accurate, earnest seekers after truth, but narrow as regards the number of such laborers.

Field experiments offer a domain in which each landowner must become his own laborer; science proper cannot enter this domain as a laborer—she can only hold the lamp of knowledge, to guide by its light, the practical farmer in his personal investigations. Science can only furnish the chart; the farmer must guide the helm, and must pass over the same course time and again, making close and accurate observations at every advance, to avoid breakers and decoys, before he can determine with certainty the true course.

The principal subjects demanding investigation, through the medium of field experiments, are

1. Experiments on worn land, with the principal elements of plant food, applied singly and in different combinations, for the purpose of determining what substances, not supplied by the soil, are needed by our various cultivated plants.

2. Experiments on lands in "good heart," or "condition," to ascertain what fertilizers produce the best results on different plants.

3. Experiments in rotation of crops, to secure the greatest possible benefit from the fertilizers applied, together with an improvement of the soil.

4. Experiments in soil fertilization, by means of leguminous plants, with lime, marl, or other mineral substances.

5. Experiments with composts of home manures, muck, etc., with phosphates, potash, etc.

6. Experiments with different varieties of our agricultural and horticultural plants.

7. Experiments with different methods of preparation

of the soil, application of fertilizers, planting and cultivation.

8. Experiments in improving seed by careful selection.

9. Experiments with different breeds of stock.

10. Experiments in feeding stock on various combinations of food.

11. Experiments in fertilizing and pruning fruit trees and vines.

12. Experiments with hedging, as a substitute for rail fences.

13. Experiments in the production of crops not yet generally cultivated.

14. Experiments in drainage and irrigation.

15. Experiments with the small industries of the farm, such as the dairy, poultry, the garden, bees etc.

The great variety of soil and climate found in Georgia renders it necessary that the same experiment be conducted in various localities, and on every variety of soil.

Many have fallen into the error of assuming that the results of experiments, conducted under circumstances widely different from those by which they are surrounded, are applicable to their localities.

Lawes and Gilbert deserve the thanks of the agricultural world for their careful, accurate, interesting, instructive and long continued field experiments, and yet we would err greatly if we accepted many of the results of their research as conclusive in our widely different surroundings.

Owing to the fact that the principal scientific and experimental investigation, and the majority of agricultural publications come to us from Europe and the northern portion of our own country under circumstances of soil and climate entirely different from our own, our reading agriculturists, following their teachings without the necessary modifications to adopt them to their immediate surroundings, fail to secure the anticipated results. More practical men avail themselves of the reading of their neighbors, apply the information gained from them with the modifications which their experience and observation teach them are necessary under the change of circumstances, and succeed. The former class are then pronounced failures, and their want of success attributed to the fact that they *learn from the books*, while the failure was not due to the fact that they read and learn from books, but from the want of the *necessary observation* and experience to enable them to make a proper application of what they learn by reading. This has been a fruitful source of the prejudice against what is called in derision "book farming."

We need, and must have, before our agriculture will take the position which its importance demands, scientific ex perimental investigation at home. Our own soil must be made to respond to well-directed specific inquiry as to its needs ; our own plants must be required to tell by increased production the kind of food and the conditions necessary for their highest development ; our own stock must answer by symetrical development and carcasses laden with flesh and fat, the kinds and combinations of food necessary for their comfort and increase, and the production of the greatest profit to their owners ; the products of our own dairies must tell in rich cream and golden butter the kind of stock to keep, the most appropriate food, and the best system of management both of the cows and the dairy products.

By whom are these experiments to be conducted ? Will farmers undertake them ? They should be conducted both by the State and by individual farmers. The State should have stations in its principal sections, the number to be determined by general differences of soil and climate, at which experiments, appropriate to each section, should be conducted ; but a large class of experiments must be conducted by farmers themselves to determine the local application of principles.

Charts should be sent out by the stations, giving not only the character of experiments to be conducted by farmers, but detailed directions, embracing a clear statement of the questions to be asked, and the precautions to be used, to make the results reliable, and the correct interpretation of the answer possible.

Perhaps the most important of the list of experiments enumerated, is that designed to ascertain what elements of plant-food required by plants, are not supplied by the soil.

On soils in good "condition," the answer to this question would not be very definite, since such have an accumulated stock of available plant-food; but on soils that are exhausted in the agricultural sense, the answer would be readily interpreted, since, in such, there is little more than their "natural strength," and the effects of different fertilizing substances, either singly or in combination, will be marked, and the results readily interpreted.

Soils that have become so far exhausted as to refuse to return remunerative crops for the labor of the husbandman, are defective in one or more of the necessary elements of plant-food in available form, which must be restored before such soils can again become productive.

They may have still remaining a sufficient supply of some of the elements in an available form, or they may be deficient in all. The problem, therefore, is to ascertain what substances are deficient in the soil. The object of experiment No. 1 is to ask nature just this question.

The farmer, in order to do this, applies to one part of the soil under investigation potash alone, to another phosphoric acid, to another nitrogen, to another potash and superphosphate, to another nitrogen and potash, to another nitrogen and phosphoric acid, to another potash, phosphoric acid and nitrogen together, to another lime, etc., with unfertilized plats between to detect any want of uniformity in the strength of the soil.

To make the experiment accurate and reliable, the preparation of the soil and the cultivation of the crop should be identical on every plat; the distribution of each fertilizer absolutely uniform throughout its plat, and the same number of plants should grow upon each.

An accurate record should be kept of the date and manner of preparation, the application of fertilizers, planting, each cultivation and the seasons; and the crop, when mature, should be gathered and accurately weighed from each plat separately. If there is an abundance of potash already in the soil, and in an available form, there will be no increase in the crop from its application; if deficient, the increased production from its use will indicate that it was needed. If the increase is still greater from the use of potash and phosphoric acid combined, this result will indicate that both of these substances were deficient in the soil. If a still greater increase results from the use of nitrogen, phosphoric acid and potash combined, this result will indicate that the soil was deficient in all three of these substances. If there is no increase of the crop, as the result of the use of any one of the substances, the indications are that the soil contained a sufficient amount of that substance for the production of the crop upon which the experiment was made.

This experiment, if carefully conducted for several years on any particular soil, will very clearly indicate what fertilizing substances are needed in that soil. It must, however, to be reliable, be conducted on each variety of soil, and by each farmer for his own information, since one soil may be deficient in one substance, and perhaps the adjoining field, or even another part of the same field, be deficient in another. Every farmer should conduct such experiments on every variety of soil on his farm. They cost but little, and may save him the expense of purchasing, in the so-called complete fertilizers, costly substances with which his land is already well supplied.

CHAPTER X.

FARM DRAINAGE.

This consists in the removal of surplus water from agricultural lands by means either of open ditches, or covered conduits, constructed a few feet below the surface of the ground.

The natural drainage of some soils is sufficient to carry off promptly all surplus water without the aid of artificial means, but where this natural drainage is, to a large extent, from the *surface*, it is extremely injurious, and often ruinous to the land.

If, however, the subsoil is sufficiently pervious to allow the surplus water to sink rapidly below the ordinary range of the roots of plants, and thence to pass freely off to streams, the natural drainage is perfect, and favorable to the growth of vegetation, unless both soil and subsoil are too coarse to admit of the rise of moisture by capillary attraction, and a reasonable atomic absorption and retention.

If the soil and subsoil are clay or loam, and the natural drainage perfect, we have the necessary conditions precedent to "high farming."

In cases where artificial drainage is necessary, the first thing to be considered is

HOW TO START.

This will depend upon the source of the evil, the topography of the surface, and the character of the subterranean strata.

The source of the evil on bottom lands is often found in numerous small springs at the base of the adjacent hills, none large enough to justify open ditches or to make useful springs. In such cases an impervious stratum of clay is usually found a few feet below the surface, which prevents the water from passing off below, and consequently causing it to saturate the soil, and even to rise and stand upon the surface.

In such cases the first duty of the land owner is to examine the ground to see if an outlet can be gotten for the drains, and what fall can be had.

Many farmers supposing that an open ditch through the center of the swamp, caused by these pent-up springs, will effectually drain it, finding their mistake after the ditch is cut, abandon the undertaking without further effort.

In order to drain such swamps, the sources of the evil must be sought out, and the water collected into underground drains at the foot of the hill, before it has an opportunity to saturate the soil below. If the substrata underlying the hills from which this water oozes are examined, there will usually be found either one of rock or impervious clay continuous under the hill, but terminating at its base.

The water, which falls upon the hills, percolates to this impervious stratum, follows its surface to its termination on the edge of the bottom, where, if not collected and carried off by ditches or underdrains, it saturates the soil and produces a swamp.

Similar oozy places, occasioned by the cropping out of impervious subterranean strata, are sometimes observed on the sides of hills, causing below them either barren galls or gullies. In all such cases the remedy must be sought in the collection of the water into underdrains before it reaches the surface, and conducting it to a main drain or open ditch.

WHERE DRAINAGE IS NECESSARY.

It is a grave mistake to suppose that only swamp lands, or those which are too wet during the whole or the greater part of the year, require drainage. All lands through which rain water is unable to percolate freely, or in which it either stands for any considerable time on the surface, or stagnates within less than three feet of the surface, will be materially benefitted by drainage.

The following extract is from "Barrall on Drainage," under the head of the "External Signs of the Want of Drainage." He says: "The aspect of the soil after heavy rains, or great protracted heat, the mode of culture, and the nature of the vegetation are very conspicuous characteristic signs, by the help of which we can easily tell that a ground needs to be drained.

"Wherever after a rain, water stays in the furrows; wherever stiff and plastic earth adheres to the shoes; wherever the foot of either man or horse makes cavities that retain water, like so many little cisterns; wherever cattle are unable to penetrate without sinking into a kind of mud; wherever the sun forms on the earth a hard crust, slightly cracked, and compressing the roots of the plants as into a vice; wherever three or four days after rain, slight depressions in the ground show more moisture than other parts; wherever a stick, forced into the ground, one foot and a half deep, forms a hole like a little well, having water standing at its bottom; wherever tradition consecrated, as advantageous, the cultivation of lands by means of convex, high, large ridges; one may affirm that drainage will produce good effects."

In addition to the above indications, the growth of certain plants known to thrive only on soils that are wet, or have stagnant water near the surface, will usually indicate to the farmer the soils that need draining.

It is frequently the case, however, that soils which are sufficiently drained, when first cleared, to produce healthy and abundant crops, become wet and sour after some years of cultivation. This has been observed, no doubt, in the experience of many farmers in Georgia.

Such soils when first cleared are drained by the roots of trees, which gradually decay, leaving ducts through which drainage water passes off to pervious strata below.

After some years of cultivation, however, these ducts become closed, and the water, unable to pass off through them, stagnates near the surface, and injures both the soil and the crops planted upon it.

The only means of restoring such lands to fertility, will be found in underdrainage.

WHAT DRAINAGE DOES.

1. *It carries off stagnant water from the surface.*—Water can only stand upon the surface of the soil when that underneath is saturated. As soon as the water is withdrawn from below, that upon the surface must descend, to obey the great hydrostatic law that water "seeks a level," until the surface is entirely relieved. If not removed by drainage, it must pass off by the slow and cooling process of evaporation. It is stated that about "four times the amount of heat is required to convert water into vapor, that is required to bring it to the boiling, from the freezing point."

Just in proportion, therefore, as the evaporation is greater from underdrained than from drained soils, is there a waste of heat.

The drainage of soils which are so wet as to cause water to stagnate on the surface, involves the conversion of absolutely useless into valuable property.

2. It *removes surplus water from under the surface*, lowering the water level to the depth at which the drains are laid.

None of our cultivated plants except, perhaps, rice, thrive on soils in which their roots find stagnant water near the surface. Besides, stagnant water seems to be no less noxious to our cultivated plants than to animal life, and, though it may supply moisture to the soil, it seems not only to be unable to supply wholesome nutrition to plants, but to contain substances which are positively injurious. The roots of plants grown upon undrained land, are therefore, compelled to occupy only that portion of the soil which lies above the water line, which is saturated in wet seasons, and baked in time of drouth. Drainage removes the surplus water, increases the area in depth which the roots may occupy, admits a free circulation of air, and, hence, a full supply of oxygen to the roots, and prevents the baking of the soil in times of drouth, while moisture and fertilizing gases are absorbed from the air. Again, the water line being lowered, rain water, impregnated with ammonia and fresh oxygen, carries these and its warmth into the soil to refresh the roots of plants. Again, as in the case of the surface water, the evaporation is reduced by the removal of the "water line" to a greater depth.

3. By removing surplus water, and lessening the evaporation from the surface, warm air and rain water are allowed free access to the depth at which the drain is laid, and consequently the soil is warmed, as well as dried, earlier in the spring, and, by affording earlier the necessary conditions of germination, the *season of growth is practically lengthened*. Every farmer has observed that gravelly or loamy soils, that are naturally underdrained, can be planted from ten to fifteen days earlier than stiff clays, which hold the surplus water from the heavy spring rains. This is just the difference between drained and undrained lands. Ten days difference in the date of maturity of two fields of wheat, will often determine the question of success or failure. Rust is the greatest enemy of the wheat crop in Georgia.

The only safeguards against this are *early maturity* and *thorough drainage*. Ten days difference in the time of planting corn will often enable the earlier planting to escape a ruinous drouth.

The market gardener who gains ten days in the maturity of his products, by having his lands thoroughly drained, will soon drive his less progressive neighbors out of the market.

4. It *deepens the soil*, by allowing the rapid percolation of water, a free circulation of air, the deep penetration of roots

of plants and insects, and facilitates chemical action in the decomposition of mineral substances, previously protected by water.

The father of drainage in America, Mr. John Johnston, of New York, said, in a communication on this subject, in 1854: "Last spring I concluded to plow a clay field, containing forty acres, only once for wheat, and that after harvest. Previous to draining, it was one of my wettest fields, and in dry weather, even in April and May, was very hard to plow, often having to get the coulters and shares sharpened every day, when we used wrought iron shares.

"Owing to the great drought before, during and after harvest, I got a large plow made, so that I could put two or more yokes of cattle and a pair of horses to it, if necessary.

"Immediately after harvest we started for the field, oxen and drivers, plowmen and horses; and, besides new shares on the plows, took other new shares along, expecting to be obliged to change every day.

"When we got to the field, I had one man put a pair of horses before the large plow, and try to open the land with a shallow furrow. He went seventy rods away and back, without even a stop, except when the clover choked the plow. I then put the plow down to eight inches, and after one round, to nearly ten, and we went around without any trouble. I then had one yoke of oxen put behind my smallest horses, and a pair of horses before each of my other plows, and they plowed the field with perfect ease, only changing shares twice.

"Although the field was undoubtedly plowed at the rate of nine inches deep, yet the clover roots went deeper, and the land plowed up as mellow as any loam; whereas, had it not been drained, it would have broke up in lumps as large as the heads of horses or oxen."

5. It *warms the soil* in spring, by allowing the rain water, which has been warmed by passing through the air, to per-

colate freely to the depth of the drain, and prevents the loss of heat incident to the slow evaporation of water stagnated in the soil or subsoil.

6. It *carries down to the roots of plants soluble plant-food*, that would, without the drainage, be carried off in surface-water to the gullies and streams.

Liquid barnyard manure, filtered through clay, comes out deprived of all coloring matters. Rain water absorbs fertilizing gases from the air during its descent, and takes up soluble matters from the surface, and carries them into the soil, where they are absorbed and retained for the use of plants.

7. It *prevents the winter-killing of small grain*, by carrying off the surplus water, which would otherwise saturate the surface soil, freeze, and break the roots of the plants.

8. It *prevents the injurious effects of drouth*, by affording a deeper range for the roots, and thus removing them from the influence of sudden changes of season. It prevents injury from drouth, also, by admitting a free circulation of air, from which moisture is condensed and absorbed by the fine particles of the soil.

9. It increases the effects of manures, by admitting their more uniform distribution through the soil, preventing their parching effects in periods of drouth, and the leaching influence of stagnant water and surface drainage, occasioned by excessive rains on undrained lands. As a result of this and other circumstances, it improves the quality and increases the quantity of the crops produced.

The most important question to be considered and determined by individuals, after a full consideration of surrounding circumstances, is,

WILL DRAINAGE PAY?

Not only individual, but general experience, in the countries that have most generally adopted underdrainage, in both field and garden, answers this question in the affirmative. It is stated that the crops of England have been doubled by drainage, and the results, as far as it has been tested, in this country, are most satisfactory. There are no known reasons why it will not pay as well in Georgia as elsewhere.

WHERE TO BEGIN.

Bottom lands, which are saturated by the water from pent-up springs, issuing from the adjacent bluffs, will naturally furnish the most conspicuous candidates for treatment, since the necessity for drainage is most obvious in such localities. The benefits derived from draining these will naturally suggest an extension of the system to uplands which are saturated and cold until late in the spring.

DRAINING MATERIAL.

Tile is, without doubt, the best material, as regards efficiency and permanence, but its cost is so great as to amount almost to prohibition. Rock is the next best, where it is accessible, and a firm botton to the drain can be had.

If the drains have a constant flow of water, so that the material will be kept *constantly wet*, *common pine poles*, from four to six inches in diameter, answer well, if the bottom of the drain is firm clay.

If the bottom is soft or sandy, it will be necessary to rest the poles upon a plank or slab, to prevent them from sinking into the ground, or the sand and mud from washing down and stopping the drain.

Three poles are required, two to rest upon the bottom of the drain, cne on each side, and the third to rest between and upon these, as represented in the accompanying figures.

The ends of the poles should be cut at right angles to the length, so as to fit well against each other, and the ends of no two poles should rest at the same

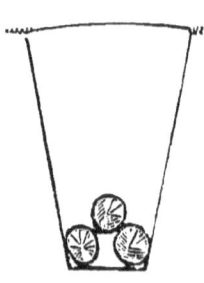

Fig. 15—*End view of Pole Drain.*

Fig. 16—*Side View of Pole Drain.*

point. The poles, after being adjusted to each other as accurately as possible, should be covered with pine straw, or some similar material, well packed down, to prevent fine earth from passing between the poles into the duct.

These poles, if kept constantly wet, will last twenty years, but if alternately wet and dry, they decay very rapidly, but will even then maintain their integrity. and make an effective drain for eight or ten years.

Trough Drains, where lumber is very cheap and accessible, answer a good purpose without foot planks, on clay bottoms, or with them on soft or sandy bottoms.

Strips one inch thick, and half of them three, and the others four inches wide, nailed together, so as to form a trough, which, inverted in the bottom of the ditch, forms a cheap and effective drain. If the bottom of the ditch is firm clay, these may rest upon the soil; if the bottom is sandy, they should rest upon a foot-plank, laid in the bottom of the ditch.

The figures 17 and 18 represent such a drain with and without the foot-plank.

The planks should be all of the same length, but put together so that one p'ank of each trough shall lap six inces over that on the opposite side of the next. (See fig. 19.) If foot-planks are used, the joints of the troughs should be placed over the centres of the former.

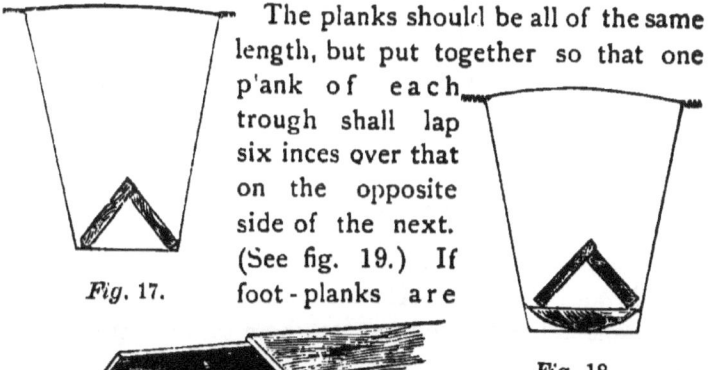

Fig. 17.

Fig. 18.

Fig. 19.

Rock-drains are expensive, unless the rock is on the surface and convenient to the proposed drain. Surface rocks that are in the way of cultivation, may be thus utilized, while they are being removed from the cultivated field.

There are several methods of utilizing rock for drainage purposes, among which are *shoulder drains*, in which a shoulder is left on each side of the bottom of the ditch, two or three inches wide, with a trench in the center three or four inches wide at the top, according to the volume of water to be discharged, and tapering to two inches in width at the bottom. This center excavation need not be more than four inches deeper than the shoulders.

Rocks are laid across the centre opening, so as to rest on the shoulders on each side, and straw, sod, or pounded rock, placed above, to exclude fine earth from the centre ditch. This kind of drain can only be used where the bottom of the ditch rests upon very firm clay.

Shed drains, in which one edge of the rock rests on one side of the bottom of the drain, and the other against the opposite side.

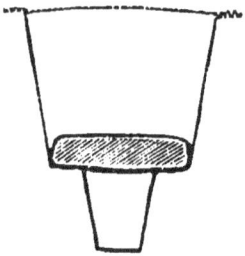

Fig. 20—Shoulder Drain. *Fig. 21—Shed Drain.*

These too will only answer in very firm clay.

Box Drains, in which rocks are set against the sides of the ditch, and others placed across them to form the roof of the drain.

For this drain the bottom of the ditch must be wider than is necessary for either the shoulder or shed drain, since it is not generally practicable to secure uniform flat rock.

If the bottom is sandy, foot-rocks must be used, to prevent the side-stones from sinking into the earth and stopping up the duct; besides, unless the bottom of the ditch is firm clay, it will wash in some parts and stagnate in others, forming deposits of sand and mud, and eventually fill up the duct.

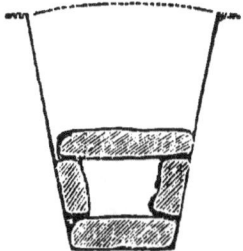 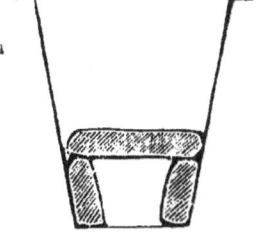

Fig. 22—*Box Drain with Foot-rock.*   Fig. 23—*Box Drain without Foot-rock.*

Pounded rock, in which the rock is broken into pieces ranging from the size of a guinea egg to that of a large hen egg, and thrown into the bottom of the ditch from six to ten inches deep. The difficulty about this drain is the danger of choking, in consequence of there being no continuous duct to carry off the water.

Tile drain, though expensive in first cost, is by far the most effective and permanent, and though the tile pipe costs more than other material, the ditch for the reception of the tile is less expensive than that for rock, poles or plank, since the bottom of the ditch need not be larger than the outside diameter of the tile used, and the top no wider than is necessary to admit the operator in opening the first two feet, the balance being dug with long-handled narrow instruments, made for the purpose, and the tile lowered by a "tile layer," the operator standing on the surface of the ground, while opening the bottom of the drain and laying the tile. The following cuts show the implements made expressly for opening drains for tile, the tile-layer, guages and span-level:

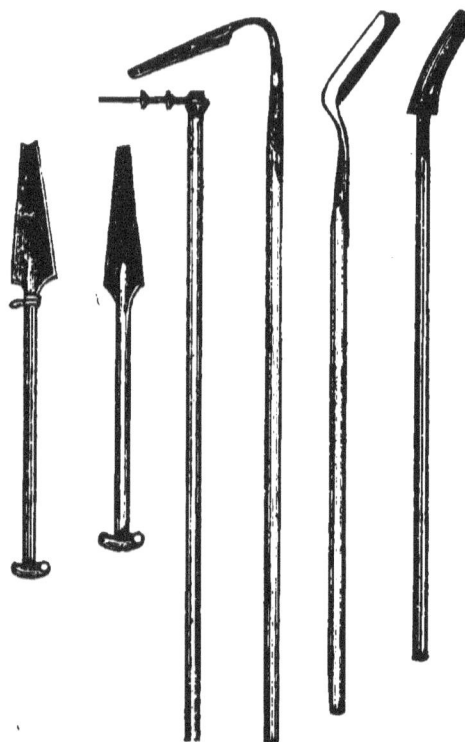

Fig. 24.

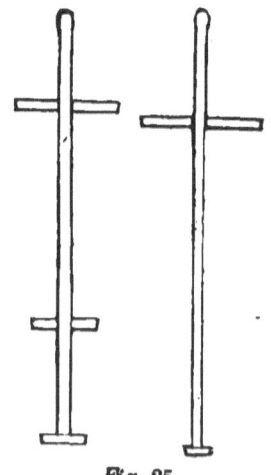

Fig. 25.

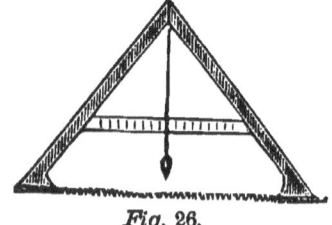

Fig. 26.

The spades and scoops explain themselves.

After the ditch is prepared for the reception of the tile, the operator, standing upon the bank, inserts the arm of the tile layer into the pipe, lowers it, and adjusts it to its place.

The gauge is used to secure uniformity in the width and depth of the drain.

The span-level is used to determine the exact fall of the drain. It is useful to ascertain the amount of fall the topography of the ground will afford, the proper location of the drains, and the uniformity of the fall in the bottom of the drain, while being dug.

Klippart, in his "Land Drainage," page 393, thus describes this useful instrument:

"Three narrow strips of board are required, each about six feet in length; these are nailed together in the form of the letter A, the span or stretch being exactly half a rod. From a nail or pin at the top, a plummet is suspended. It is then placed, for the purpose of marking, upon a floor or piece of timber, which is perfectly level, and the place where the plumb-line touches the cross-bar marked. One foot is then raised one-fourth of an inch, and the place where the line crosses the bar again marked, and will show a rise or fall of one-half inch to the rod. The foot is then raised to half an inch and the bar marked, indicating one inch to the rod. These markings can be made to any extent desired, and the instrument, by dropping it into the drain occasionally, will show that the drain is dug with uniform fall, and precisely that determined on at the outset."

This is a simple and cheap instrument, which will be found useful on the farm for other purposes than that of drainage.

Clay suitable for drain tile may be found in every section of Georgia where fine brick can be made. It should be free from pebbles, and not too poor in clay. A small amount of lime, evenly distributed through the clay, will serve as a flux in burning the tile.

If there is too much clay, the pipe will be liable to warp or crack in drying.

Machines for manufacturing drain tile cost about $250. The tile is made in pieces from one foot to eighteen inches in length Tile having 1¼ inches inside diameter cost, at present, $18.00 per thousand feet, but can be made much cheaper on the farm.

The forms principally used are the sole and the round tile. The former is objectionable on account of the liability to warp at right angles to the flat side, and thus interrupt the continuity of the fall.

While the round tile is not less liable to warp, it can be laid on the side of the warp and thus secure uniformity of fall.

They are sometimes made with unbeveled edges, and united by collars; but the cost of the latter is so great, the beveled edges are preferred.

If the inside of one end of each pipe is beveled, and the outside of the other, the union is sufficiently exact to prevent displacement, and the cost of collars avoided. The following cuts will sufficiently illustrate the different forms:

Fig. 27—Round tile with collar.   *Fig. 28—Sole tile.*

Round tile with inside bevel. Fig. 29. Same with outside bevil.

The question is often asked, "How does the water get into the pipe?" When the number of joints in a given length of 12 or 13 inch tile is considered, and that these joints cannot be made without cement (which is never used) so close as to exclude water, the question contains no difficulty.

It is estimated that, in the case of one inch pipe, "the capacity of admission at the joints more than equals the caliber of the pipe every two rods," no fear need, therefore, be entertained by those using tile pipes for drains, in reference to the water entering the pipe.

Those wishing to investigate this subject more in detail should read "Land Drainage," by Klippart, which has been freely consulted in the preparation of this chapter.

CHAPTER XI.

IRRIGATION.

In the northern half of Georgia, where there is ample fall in the water courses for the purposes of irrigation, the topography of the country is too irregular to admit of a general system of irrigation.

In the southern half there is generally insufficient fall in the streams.

Apart from these considerations, however, the necessity for irrigation will never be sufficiently felt in Georgia to induce large expenditures of money for that purpose.

By reference to the records given in the " Hand Book of Georgia," the average annual rainfall for five years, from 1871 to 1875, inclusive, at West End, near Atlanta, is found to be 53.32 inches, and that at Macon 54.88 inches.

"From observations through a long series of years, by the Smithsonian Institute, it has been found that the average annual amount of rainfall in the several sections of the State is approximately as follows: North Georgia, 50 inches; Middle and East Georgia, the northern part of southwest Georgia, and southeast Georgia, 55 inches; the middle portion of southwest Georgia, .60 inches; and the extreme southern part of southwest Georgia, 65 inches; average for the State about 54 inches."

Not only is there ample rainfall for agricultural purposes, but it is generally quite uniformly distributed through the year.

The following table, taken from the "Hand Book of Georgia," showing the rainfall for the months of June, July and August, for four years, will illustrate this point:

MONTHS	1873.			1874.			1875.			1876.		
	Rainy Days	Rain in inches		Rainy Days	Rain in inches		Rainy Days	Rain in inches		Rainy Days	Rain in inches	
June	12	2.22		14	3.85		10	3.90		14	9.12	
July	8	3.14		13	4.09		8	2.12		11	4.49	
August	10	3.58		8	3.82		9	6.95		12	6.16	
Totals	30	8.94		35	11.76		27	12.97		37	19.77	

While there is neither necessity nor probability of the adoption of any general and expensive system of irrigation in Georgia, there are many localities in which small areas may be cheaply and profitably irrigated by individual enterprise.

Notwithstanding the fact, however, that the annual rainfall throughout the State is ample, and generally well distributed through the year, there are occasional drouths of sufficient severity to render it necessary to adopt some means by which their injurious effects upon vegetation may be prevented.

By deep and thorough preparation, judicious cultivation, and the preservation of an abundant supply of humus in the soil, but little injury need result from the ordinary drouths of our summers.

CHAPTER XII.

METEOROLOGY IN ITS RELATIONS TO AGRICULTURE.

Although we have no control over either the composition of the atmosphere, or the amount or distribution of rainfall, still it is a matter of some importance that we understand the influence exerted by both upon vegetation.

The atmosphere supplies to plants nearly the whole of their organic constituents, and affords an inexhaustible source of supply, which can be neither increased nor diminished by artificial means. It is composed of oxygen and nitrogen, with small quantities of watery vapor, carbonic acid and ammonia.

Notwithstanding the very small per cent. of carbonic acid—1-1600th by weight—contained in the atmosphere, it is supposed to furnish, through the medium of the leaves and other growing parts of plants, the bulk of the carbon which makes up their cellular structure. Indeed, more than ninety per cent. of the substance of our agricultural plants is derived from the atmosphere.

Not only is carbonic acid in large quantity, and ammonia in small qnantity, absorbed through the stomata or leaf–pores, but the presence of oxygen is essential to the germination of the seed, and the growth, both of the stem and roots of plants.

Again, the fact that air brought into contact with substances colder than itself, is deprived of some of its moisture, which is condensed and deposited in the form of dew, renders the atmosphere an important source of moisture to plants, both directly, and indirectly through the medium of the soil.

Although plants probably do not absorb moisture directly from the atmosphere, the deposition of dew upon their leaves arrests evaporation, and thus diminishes the drain upon the moisture stored in the soil.

The farmer, in order to avail himself of the moisture and oxygen from the atmosphere, stirs his soil as deeply as possible, and pulverizes thoroughly, to admit a free circulation of atmospheric air. The soil cooling more rapidly than the air at night, robs the latter of its moisture, and stores it to refresh vegetation during the heat of the succeeding day.

The importance of the thorough aeration of the soil in cultivated fields is not sufficiently appreciated by our farmers.

They are too apt to consider the object of cultivation attained when the soil is freed from weeds and grass: yet a crust formed upon the surface of a cultivated field, so as to exclude the air, is more injurious to the cultivated crop than a moderate growth of weeds, accompanied with perfect aeration of the soil.

Soils differ greatly in their powers of absorbing moisture from the atmosphere.

Clay soils absorb much more than sandy, and those well supplied with humus more than those deficient in this important substance.

Underdrained soils absorb more than those whose surfaces bake from the effects of evaporation.

The absorbent power of soils is influenced by the size of the pores and the character of the particles of which it is composed. The rapidity of absorption depends upon the per cent. of moisture in the atmosphere, while the *amount* depends upon temperature. The more finely a soil is pulverized, the greater the surface exposed to the air, and consequently, the greater the absorption.

The atomic composition of the particles of soil will influence the absorption. If the particles are sand, they cannot absorb moisture, while particles of clay, composed of impalpable powder, have great absorbing power.

It is difficult to estimate the beneficial influence upon

vegetation effected by moisture absorbed by a finely pulverized soil.

The influence of the moisture of the atmosphere is well illustrated in eastern England, where the average annual rainfall is only about half that in Georgia, and yet by the absorption of moisture from the atmosphere, and the prevention of evaporation, twenty-eight inches of annual rainfall there, affords a more abundant supply of moisture to vegetation than fifty do in Georgia. Of 27.93 inches of rainfall at Rothamstead, England, 36 per cent., or 10.06 inches, percolated through 40 inches of earth, while at Waushakum farm, near Boston, Mass., only 4.76 inches out of 43.88 percolated through 25 inches of soil.

In England, 36 per cent. of the annual rainfall percolated through 40 inches of stiffish clay loam, on which no crop grew, while in Massachusetts only 11 per cent of the annual rainfall percolated through 25 inches of light gravelly loam, upon which grass grew.*

The beneficial influence of an abundance of rain and the injurious effects of an excess is well known to every farmer. The rainfall in Georgia is so well distributed throughout the year, that, with the exception of occasional periods of saturation in early spring and drouth in summer, we seldom have an excess, and generally an abundance for agricultural purposes.

The extremes are seldom so great as to be beyond the control of the skillful agriculturist.

The most interesting fact in connection with the utilization of rainfall is, that the same means viz : *Under drainage and deep tillage, serve at once to relieve the soil of surplus water and to fortify against drouth.*

A deficient amount of rainfall may be supplemented by irrigation, but this is usually accompanied by great expense, and, while it may supply *water*, it cannot effect a uniform distribution, or rob the atmosphere of its warmth

---

Scientific Farmer—Measurements from Lysimeter.

and fertilizing gases so well as a natural fall of rain. The necessity for an abundant supply of water in the soil is shown by the fact that water is the exclusive vehicle of the mineral food of plants, and that, without a certain degree of dilution of the solution of plant food in the soil, the latter becomes positively injurious. This is plainly shown in the effects of concentrated commercial fertilizers on shallow soils in times of drouth. Again, water is an essential agent, both in the decomposition of vegetable matter in the soil, and of the disintegration and chemical transformation of min eral suhstances, which, though abundant, would, without this agency, be entirely beyond the reach of vegetation.

Frost acts an important part in the preparation of mineral food for plants by the pulverization of rocks, and thus exposing their contents to the action of chemical agents. This action of frost is due to the expansion of the water which insinuates itself into the pores of solid substances, freezes, and bursts them asunder. This action exerts a beneficial influence also upon the mechanical condition of compact soils.

Evaporation, in our climate, is excessive and injurious in its effects, both upon the soil and vegetation—upon the soil, by lowering its temperature and forming a crust upon the surface, which prevents access to air; upon vegetation, by the too rapid withdrawal of watery vapor from the leaves of plants, causing the wilting and twisting of the leaves observed during periods of drouth or excessive heat.

Underdrainage, and deep and thorough pulverization of the soil, are the only practicable preventives of excessive evaporation.

Where practicable, mulching is the most effectual preventive of injurious evaporation, but it is only practicable on a small scale.

Warmth in conjunction with moisture, oxygen gas and

light, is essential to vegetation, and is required in different degrees for the normal development of different plants.

The following table taken from "How Crops Grow," shows the results of experiments conducted by Sachs to ascertain the extreme limits of warmth at which the seeds of some of the principal agricultural plants will germinate:

	Lowest Temperature.	Highest Temperature.	Temperature of Most Rapid Germination.
Wheat	41°F	104°F	84°F
Barley	41	104	84
Pea	44.5	102	84
Maize	48	115	93
Scarlet-bean	49	111	79
Squash	54	115	93

The warmth of soils is influenced by various circumstances, such as texture, color, composition, exposure, drainage, etc.

The following table taken from "How Crops Feed," shows the relative "capacity for heat" of different soils. That of lime sand being assumed as 100. Schubler heated a given volume of soil to 145°F, placed a thermometer in it and observed the time required to cool down to 70°, the temperature of the atmosphere being 61°F. In one column are stated the times of cooling, in another the *"relative power of retaining heat, or capacity for heat."*

Substance.	Time of Cooling.			Capacity for Heat.
Lime Sand	3 hours.	30	Minutes.	100
Quartz Sand	3 "	27	"	95.6
Clay Loam	2 "	30	"	71.8
Clay Plow Land	2 "	27	"	70.1
Heavy Clay	2 "	24	"	68.4
Pure Gray Clay	2 "	19	"	66.7
Garden Earth	2 "	16	"	64.8
Humus	1 "	43	"	49.0

"It will be seen that the sandy soils cool most slowly, then follows clays and heavy soils, and lastly comes humus."

The times of warming of the same soils would correspond with that of cooling if containing but little moisture and exposed to a low temperature.

Schubler found also, by experiment, that the same soils blackened and whitened, varied in temperature in about the same ratio as the surfaces of natural color did when alternately wet and dried, so that it seems that dark color exerts about the same influence upon the temperature of a soil that saturation does.

Exposure to the direct rays of the sun exerts a marked influence upon the temperature of soils that are identical in every respect. On this subject, Johnson, (in "H. C. F.,") remarks: "In the latitude of England, the sun's heat acts most powerfully on the surfaces having a southern exposure, and which are inclined at an angle of 25° and 30°. The best vineyards of the Rhine and Neckar are also on hill-sides, so situated.

"In Lapland and Spitzbergen, the southern side of hills may be seen covered with vegetation, while lasting or even perpetual snow lies on their northern inclinations."

Reflecting surfaces, such as walls and fences, especially if white, influence the temperature of the adjacent soil on the south or east side, and thus hasten the growth of vegetation. Gardeners avail themselves of such localities to forward early vegetables.

It is a source of regret that no systematic meteorological observations have been made in Georgia until recently.

Individuals in some localities have kept records of temperature and rainfall for their own information, but while these are valuable, they do not furnish sufficient data to justify deductions of general interest and utility.

A system of observations has now been inaugurated under the auspices of the Department of Agriculture, under which observations are regularly made on the temperature of the air at 7 A. M., 2 P. M., and 9 P. M., of each day, and an accurate record of both the temperature and the amount of rainfall kept. Transcripts of these records are forwarded to the Department, on the first day of each month, where the consolidated results are tabulated and published. These records are valuable as far as they go, but should, and will be made more complete. The temperature of the soil at different depths should be determined simultaneously with that of the air, the direction of the wind, at the time of each observation, should be recorded at each station, the pressure of the air should be measured by means of a standard barometer, the moisture of the atmosphere should be measured by means of the hygrometer, and the amount of percolation of rain-water measured by means of the lysimeter.

The ice has been broken—a beginning has been made, and progress both in accuracy and variety of research will necessarily follow.

These records kept for a series of years will be valuable to the agriculturists of the State, and eventually lead to instructive deductions.

CHAPTER XIII.

ENTOMOLOGY IN ITS RELATIONS TO AGRICULTURE.

The injury to vegetation resulting from the depredations of insects in the United States is estimated in millions of dollars, and yet very few farmers are able to discriminate between their friends and enemies in the insect world, for we have friends as well as enemies, among these humble inhabitants of our globe.

In every department of the animal creation we find predaceous animals which live upon their own species. Among animals we have the canines and felines; among birds, eagles, hawks. etc.; among reptiles, sharks, crocodiles, etc.; among fish, the trout and others; among insects, lady-birds, ichneumon flies, tiger-beetles, wasps, etc.

By unceasing warfare upon their enemies among animals, reptiles and birds, farmers have been able to keep them in check, and protect their friends; but the want of the necessary information in regard to the character, transformations and habits of insects, prevents a judicious discrimination between friends and foes, as well as any systematic effort to destroy the latter.

While no effort will be made to supply detailed information in regard to individual varieties, nor even of subdivisions of the orders into which insects are classified, the design of this chapter is to give to farmers a condensed statement of the principles upon which the science of Entomology is founded, the basis of the classification of insects into orders, the transformations through which those of the different orders pass from the egg to the perfect insect, and some insight into the habits of some of those insects with which the farmer meets in the prosecution of his avocation.

The Science of Entomology is based upon a thorough study of the insect world, in which specific resemblances between different insects are first observed, and those agreeing in particular characteristics grouped together and classified. The classification employed by naturalists is based principally upon the structure of the mouth, in the adult state, the structure and number of the wings, and the transformations which the insects undergo in passing from the egg to the adult state.

The first great divisions are called *orders*, of which some naturalists give seven and others eight :

They are—

1. "COLEOPTERA (*sheath-winged*). (Beetles). Insects with jaws, two thick wing covers meeting in a straight line on the top of the back, and two filmy wings, which are folded transversely. Transformation complete. Larvæ called grubs, generally provided with six true legs, and sometimes also with a terminal prop-leg; more rarely without legs. Pupa, with the wings and legs distinct and unconfined." Some of the coleoptera are friends to man; such

as the lady-birds, tiger-beetles, predaceous ground-beetles, and some others, which destroy caterpillars, plant-lice, and other insects injurious to vegetation. Others serve as scavengers, by the removal of carrion, dung, and other filth. Others live altogether on the mushroom family of plants; others live under the bark of trees, and in the trunks of old trees, and are injurious, but many of them living mainly upon dead or decayed bark and wood, oo but little damage.

There are others still, called blistering beetles (cantharididæ), which are employed in the healing art.

2. "ORTHOPTERA (*straight-winged*). (Cockroaches, crickets, grasshoppers, etc). Insects with jaws, two rather thick and opaque upper wings, overlapping a little on the back, and two larger, thin wings, which are folded in plaits, like a fan. Transformation partial. Larvæ and pupæ active, but wanting wings." With one exception, all of the orthoptera are injurious, either to household goods or vegetation.

Their larvæ closely resemble the perfect insect, and their pupæ do not lie in an apparently dormant state like those of the Coleoptera, Lepidoptera, etc., though they shed their skins usually six times during their transformation from the larva to the perfect insect. Unlike insects which undergo a complete transformation, they continue to grow during their transformation, increasing in voracity with their advancement towards maturity, and, unlike the Lepidoptera, continuing their depredations after maturity.

Orthoptera are subdivided into—

1st. *Runners*, such as earwigs and cockroaches, which are provided with legs suited for rapid motion :

2d. *Graspers*, embracing mantes or soothsayers, which have teeth on their forelegs suited to grasping other insects, upon which they prey.

3d. *Walkers*, such as "walking-sticks," which have long

slender legs, capable only of slow motion. They live upon the tender parts of plants.

4th. *Jumpers*, as crickets, locusts and grasshoppers, whose hind legs are longer than the others, and adapted to quick and long leaping.

This is the most prolific, as well as the most destructive, of the Orthoptera. Some of the crickets prey upon other insects, but the principal food of the jumpers consists of the green parts of plants.

4. "HEMIPTERA (*bugs, locusts, plant-lice, etc.*) Insects with a horney beak for suction, four wings, whereof the uppermost are generally thick at the base, with thinner extremities, which are flat, and cross each other on the top of the back, or are of uniform thickness throughout, and slope at the sides like a roof. Transformation partial. Larvæ and pupæ nearly like the adult insect, but wanting wings."

Some of the field and house bugs of this order emit very offensive odors, when disturbed. Some live on the juices of animals, and destroy vast numbers of noxious insects. Others are useful in supplying dye-stuffs of great value in the arts.

Others, embracing plant-bugs, plant-lice, bark-lice, mealy bugs, etc., that suck the juices of plants, are very injurious, and difficult to destroy.

5. "NEUROPTERA (*dragon-flies, lace-winged flies, May-flies, ant-lions, day-flies, white ants etc.*) Insects with jaws, four netted wings, of which the hinder ones are the largest, and no sting or piercer. Transformation complete or partial. Larvæ or pupæ various."

Many of this order prey upon other insects both in their larvæ and adult states. Dragon-flies are especially useful in destroying gnats and mosquitoes. The lace-winged flies, in the larva state, destroy great numbers of plant-lice.

6. "LEPIDOPTERA—*scale-winged, (butter flies and moths.*) Mouth with a spiral sucking tube, wings four, covered with brawny scales. Transformation complete. The larvæ

are caterpillars, and have six true legs, and from four to ten fleshy prop-legs. Pupæ with the cases of the wings and of the legs indistinct and soldered to the breast."

"Some kinds of caterpillars are domestic pests, and devour cloth, wool, furs, feathers, wax, lard, flour and the like; but by far the greatest number live wholly on vegetable food, certain kinds being exclusively leaf-eaters, while others attack the buds, fruit, seeds, bark, pith, stems and roots of plants."

Insects of this order are by far the most injurious, both as domestic pests and as destroyers of vegetation. They pass through four stages, viz: the egg, the larva, pupa and imago, or perfect insect. The instincts of these insects teach them to deposit their eggs where the larvæ, the only state in which they are injurious, will have appropriate food as soon as they are hatched. This is illustrated by the conduct of the tobacco fly, which deposits its eggs upon the leaf of the tobacco, tomato, or other plants upon which the larvæ feed; the cotton moth, which deposits its eggs upon the leaf of the cotton plant, and the moth of the corn worm, which deposits its eggs upon the tender bud of the stalk, or the young ears of corn.

One of the most remarkable evidences of this instinct is shown by the tent caterpillar, which deposits its eggs in the fall upon the small limbs of those trees which are among the earliest to put forth their leaves in spring. The observant farmer has noticed the partiality of the moth of this caterpillar for the wild crab apple tree which grows in our forests, and, also, that this is the first tree in the forests to put forth its leaves in spring. This is the caterpillar which webs in the forks of apple trees in spring, and preys upon the young leaves as soon as they appear. In the fall it is seen in great numbers on the persimmon trees.

The cutworm, so destructive in garden and field in spring, belongs to this order. Indeed, the worst enemies to our cultivated plants are found among the Lepidoptera.

It is important that farmers become familiar with the butterflies and moths which lay the eggs of the caterpillars which are most destructive to vegetation, as well as their habits, in order that the means necessary for their destruction may be used.

Tobacco growers destroy great numbers of the tobacco fly by poisoning with cobalt the flowers of the stramonium (commonly known as Jamestown weed) upon which the fly feeds at night.

Since each female usually lays from 200 to 500 eggs, the importance of destroying the adult insect, if possible rather than the larvæ, is apparent. The difficulty attending the destruction of the fly or moth renders warfare upon the caterpillar necessary.

The principle distinction between the butterflies and moths is found in the antennæ, the position of the wings when at rest, the hind legs, and the times at which they are active.

Butterflies have thread-like antennæ with knobs at the end, have two little spurs on the hind legs, fold their wings back to back, when at rest, and fly only by day.

Hawk-moths have the antennæ thickened in the middle, and tapering at each end, wings inclined like a roof when at rest, and hind legs with two pairs of spurs. Some fly by day, but the majority of them only in the morning and evening twilight.

Moths have antennæ tapering from the base to the extremity, have two pairs of spurs on their hind legs, wings sloping when at rest, and fly mostly by night.

Many of the night-flyers may be destroyed by fires kept up for a few hours, beginning with early twilight.

6. "HEMENOPTERA (*saw flies, ants, wasps, bees, etc.*) Insects with jaws, four veined wings, in most species the hinder pair being the smallest, and a piercer or sting at the extremity of the abdomen. Transformation complete. Larvæ mostly maggot-like, or slug-like; of some, caterpillar like. Pupæ with the legs and wings unconfined."

In this order are found insects both beneficial and injurious to the interests of man. Among them we find leaf-eaters, pine-borers and gall-flies that are injurious; while on the other hand, there are the ichneumon, flies, ants and wasps, which prey upon other insects, and the useful little bee, which labors so persistently in laying up his stores, which are appropriated by man to his own use. The bees and other insects also serve the important purpose of fertilizing the flowers of plants, by carrying the pollen from blossom to blossom, in their search for honey.

7. "DIPTERA." (*Mosquitoes, gnats, flies, etc*). Insects with a horny or fleshy proboscis, two wings only, and two knobbed threads, called balances or poiser, behind the wings. Transformation complete. The larvæ are maggots, without feet, and with the breathing holes generally in the hinder extremity of the body. Pupæ mostly incased in the dried skin of the larvæ, sometimes, however, naked, in which case the wings and legs are visible, and are found to be more or less free or unconfined." In this order are several species which are extremely annoying to man in summer, such as mosquitoes, gnats, and various kinds of flies, including the house fly, blow-flies, flesh-flies, and the cheese fly, which produces skippers.

Among those injurious to vegetation we find the Hessian fly, so destructive in its larva state to wheat. There are still others, which have no common name, which deposit their eggs among plant lice or in the nests of other insects, where they either destroy the young, or subsist upon the food stored up for the use of the young when hatched, and thus starve them to death.

These seven orders embrace with sufficient accuracy those insects which from their injury or benefit to man, require the attention of agriculturists.

The limit to which this work is necessarily circumscribed, forbids the enumeration of the subdivisions of these orders, or detailed descriptions of individual varieties.

The importance, to farmers, of some knowledge of the classification, transformations and habits of insects injurious to vegetation, and the necessity for the means of distinguishing between friends and enemies, rendered it proper that the subject should not be omitted in a work of this character.

If what has been written shall have the effect of stimulating careful and accurate observation and investigation of insects on the part of the farmers of the State, its principal object will have been accomplished. Any farmer who will review his experience, and estimate the injury to his crops by insects during the last decade, will be forced to appreciate the importance of utilizing the information supplied by the science of Entomology.

"Insects Injurious to Vegetation," by Harris, has been freely quoted, and information derived from it utilized. Those desiring more detailed information to aid them in heir investigations, will do well to secure this work.

In the preparation of this work, the following works have been freely consulted, viz: How Crops Grow and How Crops Feed—Prof. S. W. Johnson; Scientific Agriculture—Prof. E. M. Pendleton; Elements of Agriculture, Chemistry and Geology—Prof. F. W. Johnston; Talks on Manures—Mr. Joseph Harris; Land Drainage—Prof. John H. Klippart; Structural and Systematic Botany—Prof. Asa Gray. The principal engravings have been copied from Johnson, Gray and Klippart.

APPENDIX.

For convenience of reference, the following tables are copied from "Talks on Manures," by Harris. Mr. Harris says of them: "The following tables of analyses are copied in full from the last edition (1875) of Dr. Emil Wolff's *Pracktische Dungerlehre*.

"The figures differ materially, in many cases, from those previously published. They represent the average results of numerous reliable analyses, and are sufficiently accurate for all practical purposes connected with the subject of manures:

In special cases, it will be well to consult actual analyses of the articles to be used."

I—TABLES FOR CALCULATING THE EXHAUSTION AND ENRICHING OF SOILS.

A.—HARVEST PRODUCTS AND VARIOUS MANUFACTURED ARTICLES.

Average quantity of water, nitrogen, and total ash, and the different ingredients of the ash in 1,000 lbs. of fresh or air-dried substance.

Substance.	Water.	Nitrogen.	Ash.	Potash.	Soda.	Lime.	Magnesia.	Phosphoric Acid.	Sulphuric Acid.	Silica and Sand.
I—.HAY.										
Meadow Hay...............	143	15.5	51.5	13.2	2.3	8.6	3.3	4.1	2.4	13.9
Rye Grass...............	143	16.3	53.2	20.2	2.0	4.3	1.3	6.2	2.3	18.5
Timothy...............	143	15.5	62.1	20.4	1.5	4.5	1.9	7.2	1.8	22.1
Red Clover...............	160	19.7	56.9	18.3	1.2	20.0	6.1	5.6	1.7	1.4
Red Clover, ripe.........	150	12.5	44.0	9.8	1.4	15.6	6.8	4.3	1.3	3.0
White Clover............	165	23.2	59.8	16.1	4.5	19.3	6.0	8.4	4.0	2.5
Alsike Clover............	160	24.0	39.7	11.0	1.2	13.5	5.0	4.0	1.6	1.6
Crimson Clover.........	167	19.5	50.7	11.7	4.3	16.0	3.1	3.6	1.3	8.2
Lucern...................	160	23.0	62.1	15.3	1.3	26.2	3.3	5.5	3.7	8.8
Esparsette...............	167	21.3	45.8	13.0	1.5	16.8	3.0	4.6	1.4	3.7
Yellow Clover...........	167	22.1	55.7	11.9	1.3	32.6	2.1	4.3	1.0	1.5
Green Vetch Hay......	167	22.7	83.7	28.3	5.6	22.8	5.4	10 7	2.8	4.9
Green Pea Hay..........	167	22.9	62.4	28.2	2.8	15.6	6.3	6.8	5.1	0.9
Spurrey..................	167	19.2	56.8	19.9	4.6	10.9	6.9	8.4	2.0	0.8
II.—GREEN FODDER.										
Meadow Grass in bloom..................	700	5.4	18.1	4.6	0.8	3.0	1.1	1.5	0.3	4.9
Young Grass...........	800	5.6	20.7	11.6	0.4	2.2	0.6	2.2	0.8	2.1
Rye Grass...............	734	5.7	20.4	7.2	0.7	1.5	0.4	2.2	0 8	6.5
Timothy Grass.........	700	5.4	21.6	7.4	0 5	1.6	0.7	2.5	0.6	7.7
Rye-Fodder.............	760	5.3	16.3	6.3	0.1	1.2	0 5	2.4	0 2	5.2
Green Oats...............	810	3.7	18.8	7 5	0.6	1.2	0.6	1.7	0.6	5.7
Green Corn-Fodder...	822	1.9	12.0	4.3	0.5	1.6	1.4	1.3	0.4	1.7
Sorghum.................	773	4.0	13.0	3.6	1.8	1.2	0.5	0.8	0 4	3.7
Moharbay.................	700	5.9	13.9	5.0	0.3	1.4	1.3	0.8	0.5	3.9
Red Clover in blossom	780	5.1	13.7	4.4	0.3	4 8	1.5	1.4	0.4	0.3
" " before "	830	5.3	14.5	5.3	0.3	4.2	1.5	1.7	0.3	0 4
White Clover...........	805	5.6	13.6	2.8	1.0	4.4	1.4	1.9	1.1	0.6
Alsike Clover...........	820	5.3	8.8	6 4	0.3	3.0	1.1	0.9	0.4	0.4
Crimson Clover.........	815	4.3	12.2	2.8	1.0	3.8	0.7	0.9	0.3	2.0
Lucern...................	740	7.2	18.7	4.6	0.4	7.9	1.0	1.6	1.1	1.1
Esparsette...............	80)	5.1	12.1	3.4	0.4	4.4	0.8	1.2	0.4	1.0
Yellow Clover...........	830	4.5	14.7	3.2	0.3	8.6	0.6	1.1	0.3	0.4
Green Vetch.............	820	5 6	18.1	6 1	1.2	4.9	1.2	2.3	0.6	1.1
Green Peas...............	815	5.1	13.9	5.1	0 5	3.5	1.4	1.5	1.1	0.2
Green Rape.............	870	4.6	12.2	4.0	0 4	2.7	0.5	1.4	1.7	0.6
Spurrey..................	800	3.7	12.2	4.3	1.0	2.3	1.5	1.8	0.4	0.2
III.—ROOT CROPS.										
Potatoes.................	750	3.4	9.4	5.7	0.2	0.2	0.4	1.6	0.6	0.2
Jerusalem Artichoke.	800	3.2	9.8	4.7	1.0	0.3	0.3	1.4	0·5	1.0
Mangel-wurzel.........	880	1.8	7.5	4.1	1.2	0.3	0.3	0.6	0.2	0.2
Sugar Beets............	815	1.6	7.1	3.9	0.7	0.4	0.5	0 8	0.3	0.1
Turnips..................	920	1.8	7.3	3.3	0.7	0.8	0.3	0.9	0.8	0.1
Carrots...................	850	2.2	7.8	2.8	1.7	0.9	0 4	1.0	0 5	0.2
Russia Turnips.........	870	2.1	11.6	4.7	1.2	1.3	0.3	1.7	1.5	0.1
Chiccory.................	800	2.5	6.7	2.6	1.1	0.5	0.5	0.8	0.5	0.3
Sugar Beet, upper part of root...............	840	2.0	9.6	2.8	2.3	0.9	1.1	1.2	0.7	0.2

Substance.	Water.	Nitrogen.	Ash.	Potash.	Soda.	Lime.	Magnesia.	Phosphoric Acid.	Sulphuric Acid.	Silica and Sand.
IV.—Leaves & Stems of Root Crops.										
Potato Vines, nearly ripe	770	4.9	19.7	4.3	0.4	6.4	3.3	1.6	1.3	0.9
Potato Vines, unripe	825	6.3	16.5	4.4	0.3	5.1	2.4	1.2	0.8	1.2
Jerusalem Artichoke	800	5.3	14.5	3.1	0.2	5.0	1.3	0.7	0.2	3.6
Mangel-wurzel	905	3.0	14.1	4.1	2.9	1.6	1.3	0.8	0.8	0.5
Sugar Beets	897	8.0	18.1	6.5	2.7	2.7	2.7	1.3	0.9	0.7
Turnips	898	3.0	11.9	2.8	1.1	3.9	0.5	0.9	1.1	0.5
Carrots	822	5.1	26.0	2.9	5.2	8.5	0.9	1.2	2.0	2.9
Chiccory	830	3.5	16.5	4.3	2.9	8.2	0.4	1.0	1.4	0.6
Russia Turnips	850	4.6	25.3	3.7	1.0	8.4	1.0	2.6	3.0	2.6
Cabbage, white	890	2.4	16.0	6.3	0.9	3.1	0.6	1.4	2.4	0.2
Cabbage Stems	820	1.8	11.6	5.1	0.6	1.3	0.5	2.4	0.9	0.2
V.—Manufactured Products & Refuse.										
Wheat Bran	131	22.4	53.5	14.3	0.2	1.7	8.8	27.3	0.1	0.5
Rye Bran	125	23.2	71.4	19.3	1.0	2.5	11.3	34.3		1.4
Barley Bran	120	23.7	48.4	8.1	0.7	1.8	3.0	8.9	0.9	23.6
Oat Hulls	140		34.7	4.9	0.8	1.4	1.0	1.6	1.3	23.3
Pea Bran	140		22.7	10.3	0.2	4.1	2.2	3.1	0.9	0.9
Buckwheat Bran	140	27.2	34.6	11.2	0.7	3.4	4.6	12.5	1.0	0.7
Wheat Flour	136	18.9	7.2	2.6	0.1	0.2	0.1	3.7		
Rye Flour	142	16.8	16.9	6.5	0.3	0.2	1.4	8.5		
Barley Meal	140	16.0	20.0	5.8	0.5	0.6	2.7	9.5	0.6	
Corn Meal	140	16.0	5.9	1.7	0.2	0.4	0.9	2.6		
Green Malt	476	10.4	14.6	2.5		0.5	1.2	5.3		4.8
Dry Malt	75	16.0	26.6	4.6		1.0	2.2	9.7		8.8
Brewer's Grains	766	7.8	11.7	0.5	0.1	1.3	1.0	4.1		4.6
Beer	900		6.2	2.1	0.6	0.2	0.4	2.0	0.2	0.6
Malt sprouts	80	36.8	66.7	20.6	1.2	1.9	1.8	18.0	2.9	14.7
Potato Fibre	850	1.3	1.8	0.3		0.9	0.1	0.4		0.1
Potato Slump	948	1.6	5.0	2.2	0.4	0.3	0.4	1.0	0.4	0.2
Sugar-beet Pomace	700	2.9	11.4	3.9	0.9	2.6	0.7	1.1	0.4	0.9
Clarifying Refuse	948	0.8	3.3	0.8	0.1	1.1	0.2	0.2	0.1	0.7
Sugar-beet Molasses	172	12.8	82.3	57.5	10.0	4.7	0.3	0.5	1.7	0.3
Molasses Slump	920	3.2	14.0	11.0	1.5	0.2		0.1	0.2	
Rape-cake	150	48.5	54.6	12.4	1.8	6.8	7.0	19.2	3.2	2.8
Linseed Oil-cake	115	45.3	50.8	12.4	0.7	4.3	8.5	16.1	1.6	6.4
Poppy-cake	100	52.0	76.9	2.3	2.3	27.0	6.2	31.2	1.9	4.5
Beach-nut-cake	100	38.1	43.8	6.5	4.6	13.2	8.6	9.7	0.6	0.8
Walnut-cake	137	55.3	46.2	14.3		3.1	5.6	20.2	0.6	0.7
Cotton-seed-cake	115	39.0	58.4	14.6		2.7	8.9	28.1	0.7	2.3
Coconut-cake	127	87.4	55.1	22.4	1.3	2.6	1.6	14.9	2.1	1.9
Palm-oil-cake	100	25.9	26.1	5.0	0.2	3.1	4.5	11.0	0.5	0.8
VI.—Straw.										
Winter Wheat	143	4.8	46.1	6.3	0.6	2.7	1.1	2.2	1.1	31.2
Winter Spelt	143	4.0	50.1	5.2	0.3	2.9	1.2	2.6	1.2	36.0
Winter Rye	143	4.0	40.5	7.8	0.9	3.5	1.1	2.1	1.1	22.9
Spring Wheat	143	5.6	38.1	11.0	1.0	2.6	0.9	2.0	1.2	18.2
Spring Rye	143	5.6	46.6	11.2		4.2	1.8	3.0	1.2	26.1
Barley	143	6.4	41.3	9.4	1.7	3.2	1.1	1.9	1.5	21.5
Oats	143	5.6	40.4	8.9	1.2	3.6	1.6	1.9	1.3	19.6
Indian Corn-stalks	150	4.8	41.9	9.6	0.1	4.0	2.6	5.3	1.1	11.7
Buckwheat Straw	160	13.0	51.7	24.2	1.1	9.5	1.9	6.1	2.7	2.9
Pea Straw	160	10.4	44.0	10.1	1.8	16.2	3.5	3.5	2.7	8.0
Field Bean	160	16.3	43.9	18.5	1.1	9.8	3.3	3.2	1.6	3.2
Garden Bean	160		40.0	12.8	3.2	11.1	2.5	3.9	1.7	1.9
Common Vetch	160	12.0	44.1	6.8	6.9	15.6	3.7	2.7	3.2	3.6
Lupine	160	9.4	41.4	8.0	2.6	14.8	3.6	3.7	3.0	2.1
Rape	160	5.6	40.8	11.1	3.8	11.6	2.5	2.4	3.1	2.6
Poppy	160		48.7	18.4	0.6	14.7	3.1	1.6	2.5	5.5

Substance.	Water.	Nitrogen.	Ash.	Potash.	Soda.	Lime.	Magnesia.	Phosphoric Acid.	Sulphuric Acid.	Silica and Sand.
VII.—CHAFF.										
Winter Wheat	143	7.2	92.5	8.5	1.7	1.8	1.2	4.0		75.1
Spring Wheat	143	7 5	121.4	4.8	1.0	4.0	1.5	3.1	0.7	105.3
Winter Spelt	143	5.6	82.7	7.9	0.2	2.0	2.1	6.1	1.9	61.3
Winter Rye	143	5 8	84.0	5.3	0.3	3.5	1.2	5.6	0.1	69.2
Barley Awns	143	4.8	120.0	9.4	1.2	12.7	1.6	2.4	3.7	86.6
Oats	143	6.4	71.2	4.6	2.9	4.0	1.5	1.3	3.5	50.4
Indian Corn-cobs	140	2.3	4.6	2.4	0.1	0.2	0.2	0.2	0 1	1.3
Field Beans	150	16.8	54.5	35.3	1.3	6.8	5.9	2.7	1.2	0.3
Lupine	143	7.2	18.1	8.7	0.7	3.6	1.5	1.1	0.5	0.0
Rape.	140	6.4	73.2	11.8	4.4	36·3	4.2	3.4	7.3	1 0
Flax-seed Hulls	120		54.7	15.4	3·0	15.4	3.3	4.5	3.4	5.0
VIII.—COMMERCIAL PLANTS, ETC.										
Flax Stems	140		30.4	9.4	2.5	6.8	2.0	4.0	2.0	1.7
Rotted Flax Stems	100		7.0	0.3	0.2	3.6	0.2	0.8	0.2	1.3
Flax Fibre	100		6.8	0.3	0.3	3.6	0.3	0 7	0.3	0.6
Hemp Stems	150		33 2	4·6	0.7	20.3	2.4	2.3	0.7	3.5
Hops, entire plant	140		81.4	20.1	2.8	18.1	6.4	7.5	3.7	16.4
Hops	120		66 8	23.0	1.4	11.1	3.7	11.2	2.4	11.1
Hop Stems	160		40.7	11.4	1.7	12.6	2.7	4.4	1.3	3.4
Tobacco Leaves	180		151.0	30.3	5.1	62.8	17.7	4.8	5.8	13.5
Wine and Must	866		2.1	1.3		0.1	0.1	0.4	0.1	
Wine-grounds	650		13.9	6.1	0.2	2.9	0.7	2.5	0.6	0.2
Grape Stems, etc	530		13.0	4.0	1.4	4.5	0.7	1.6	0.3	0.2
Mulberry Leaves	850		16.3	8.9	0.2	5.4	1.0	1.3	0.3	4.1
IX.—MATERIALS FOR BEDDING.										
Reed	180		36.7	6.8	0 2	3.3	1.1	2.3	0.6	20.0
Sedge Grass	140		61.2	17.7	4.9	4.2	2.9	4.6	2 3	20.3
Rush	140		48.1	19.0	3.1	3.6	3.1	4.3	1.3	6.8
Beech Leaves, August	560		19.0	3.7	0.4	6 4	1.4	1.8	0,4	3.8
" " Autumn	150	8.0	58.5	2.3	0.4	26.4	3.5	2.4	2.1	19.7
Oak Leaves, August	550		15.8	5.4		4.1	2.1	1.9	0.4	0.7
" " Autumn	150	8 0	41.7	1.4	0.3	20.3	1.7	3.5	1.8	12.9
Fir Needles	475	5.0	18.4	1.0	0.3	6.1	1.1	1.0	0.4	6.3
Pine Needles	450		32.0	0.6	0.1	4.3	0.5	1.4	0.6	22.6
Moss	250		19.2	2.6	1.6	2.2	1.1	0.9	1.0	5.5
Fern	250		50.7	18.0	2.1	6.2	3.5	4.2	1.8	10.3
Heath	200	10.0	16.6	2.1	1.1	3.6	1.6	1.1	0.7	4.9
Broom	250		13.6	4.8	0.3	2 2	1.6	1.1	0.4	1.3
Sea-Weed	150	14.0	122.3	15.9	28.1	16.7	10.0	8.8	26.3	2.5
X.—GRAINS AND SEEDS.										
Winter Wheat	144	20.8	16.9	5.8	0.4	0.6	2.0	7.9	0.1	0.4
Spring Wheat	143	20.5	18.8	5.5	0.4	0.5	2.2	8.9	0,3	0.3
Spelt, without husk	143	22.0	14.2	5.1	0.5	0.4	1.7	6.0		0.2
Spelt, with husk	148	16.0	36.6	5.7	0·4	1.0	2.4	7.6	1.1	17.1
Winter Rye	143	17.6	17.9	5.6	0.3	0.5	2.1	8.4	0.2	0.4
Winter Barley	145	16.0	17.0	2.6	0.7	0.2	2.1	5.6	0.5	4.9
Spring Barley	143	16.0	22.2	4·5	0.6	0.6	1·9	7.7	0.4	6.1
Oats	143	19.2	27.0	4.4	0.6	1.0	1.9	6.2	0.4	12.0
Millet	140	20.3	29.8	8.4	0.4	0.2	2.9	5.9	0.1	15.8
Indian Corn	144	16.0	13.0	3.7	0.2	0.3	2.0	5.9	0.2	0.2
Sorghum	140		16.0	3.3	0.5	0.2	2.4	8.1		1.2
Buckwheat	140	14.4	11.8	2.7	0.7	0.5	1.5	5 7	0 2	0.1
Peas	143	35.8	28.5	9.8	0.2	1.2	1.9	8.6	0.8	0.2
Field Beans	145	40.8	30.7	13.1	0.4	1.5	2.2	11 9	0.8	0.2
Garden Beans	150	39.0	27.4	12.0	0.4	1.8	2.0	9.7	1.1	0.2

Substance.	Water.	Nitrogen.	Ash.	Potash.	Soda.	Lime.	Magnesia.	Phosphoric Acid.	Sulphuric Acid.	Silica and Sand.
Vetch	143	44.0	26.8	8.1	2.1	2.1	2.4	10.0	1.0	0.3
Lupine	130	56.6	34.1	10.2	0.1	3.0	4.0	14.3	1.5	0.2
Red Clover	150	30.5	39.3	13.5	0.4	2.5	4.9	14.5	0.9	0.5
White Clover	150		33.8	12.3	0.2	2.5	3.9	11.6	1.6	0.8
Esparsette	160		38.4	11.0	1.1	12.3	2.6	9-2	1.2	0.3
Ruta-bagas	140		43.8	9.1	8.5	7.6	8.6	7.6	2.1	1.1
Sugar-Beet	146		45.1	11.1	4.2	10·2	7.3	7.5	2.0	0.8
Carrots	120		74.8	14.3	3.5	29.1	5.0	11.8	4.2	4.0
Chiccory	130		54.6	6.5	4.6	17.3	5.9	16.5	2.4	0.6
Turnips	125		34.6	7.6	0.4	6.1	3.1	14.0	2.5	0.2
Rape	118	31.2	39.1	9.6	0.6	5.5	4.6	16.5	0.9	0.5
Summer-Rape	120		34.9	7.7		5.2	4.7	14.9	2.8	
Mustard	130		36.5	5.9	2.0	7.0	3.7	14.6	1.8	0.9
Poppy	147	28.0	52.9	7.2	0.5	18.7	5.0	10.6	1.0	1.7
Linseed	118	32.8	32.6	10.0	0.7	2.6	4.7	13.5	0.8	0.4
Hemp	122	26.1	45.3	9.4	0.4	10.9	2.6	16.9	0.1	5.5
Grape-seeds	110		25.0	7.2		8.4	2.1	6.0	0.6	0.3
Horse-chestnuts, fresh	492	10.2	12.0	7.1		1.4	0.1	2.7	0.3	0.3
Acorns, fresh	560		9.6	6.2	0.1	0.7	0.5	1.4	0.4	0.1
XI.—Various Animal Products.										
Cows' Milk	875	5.1	6.2	1.5	0.6	1.3	0.2	1.7		
Sheep Milk	860	5.5	8.4	1·8	0.3	2.5	0.1	3.0	0.1	0.2
Cheese	450	45.3	67.4	2.5	26.6	6.9	0.2	11.5		
Ox-blood	790	32.0	7.5	0.6	3.4	0.1	0.1	0.4	0.2	0.1
Calf-blood	800	29.0	7.1	0.8	2.9	0.1	0.1	0.6	0.1	
Sheep-blood	790	32.0	7.5	0.5	3.3	0.1	0.1	0.4	0.1	
Swine-blood	800	29.0	7.1	1.5	2.2	0.1	0.1	0.9	0.1	
Ox-flesh	770	36.0	12.6	5.2		0.2	0.4	4.3	0.4	0.3
Calf-flesh	780	34.9	12.0	4.1	1.0	0.2	0.2	5.8		0.1
Swine-flesh	740	34.7	10.4	3.9	0.5	0.8	0.5	4.6		
Living Ox	597	26.6	46·6	1.7	1.4	20.8	0.6	18.6		0.1
Living Calf	662	25.0	38.0	2.4	0.6	16.3	0.5	13.8		0.1
Living Sheep	591	22.4	31.7	1.5	1.4	13.2	0.4	12.3		0.2
Living Swine	528	20.0	21.6	1.8	0.2	9.2	0.4	8.8		
Eggs	672	21.8	61.8	1.5	1.4	54.0	1.0	8.7	0.1	0.1
Wool, washed	120	94.4	9.7	1.8	0.3	2.4	0.6	0.3		2.5
Wool, unwashed	150	54.0	98.8	74.6	1.9	4.2	1.6	1.1	4.0	3.0

B.—AVERAGE COMPOSITION OF VARIOUS MANURES.

Name of Fertilizer.	Water.	Organic Substance.	Ash.	Nitrogen.	Potash.	Soda.	Lime.	Magnesia.	Phosphoric Acid	Sulphuric Acid	Silica and Sand.	Chlorine & Fluorine
I.—ANIMAL EXCREMENTS.												
(In 100 parts of Manure.)												
Fresh Fæces:												
Horse	757	211	31.6	4.4	3.5	0.6	1.5	1.2	3.5	0.6	19.6	0.2
Cattle	838	145	17.2	2.9	1.0	0.2	3.4	1.3	1.7	0.4	7.2	0.2
Sheep	655	314	31.1	5.5	1.5	1 0	4.6	1.5	3.1	1.4	17.5	0 3
Swine	820	150	30.0	6.0	2.6	2.5	0.9	1.0	4.1	0 4	15.0	0.3
Fresh Urine:												
Horse	901	71	29.0	15.5	15.0	2.5	4.5	2 4		0 6	0.8	1.5
Cattle	938	35	27.4	5.8	4.9	6.4	0.1	0.4		1.3	0.3	3.8
Sheep	872	83	45.2	19.5	22.6	5.4	1.6	3.4	0.1	3.0	0.1	6.5
Swine	967	28	15.0	4.3	8.3	2.1		0.8	0.7	0.8		2.3
Fresh Dung (with straw):*												
Horse	713	254	32.6	5.8	5 3	1.0	2.1	1.4	2.8	0 7	17.7	0.4
Cattle	775	203	21.8	3.4	4.0	1.4	3.1	1.1	1.6	0.6	8.5	1.0
Sheep	646	318	35.6	8.3	6.7	2.2	3.3	1.8	2.3	1.5	14.7	1.7
Swine	724	250	25.6	4.5	6.0	2.0	0.8	0.9	1.9	0.8	10.8	1.7
Common Barn-yard Manure:												
Fresh	710	246	44.1	4 5	5.2	1.5	5.7	1.4	2.1	1 2	12.5	1.5
Moderately rotted	750	192	58.0	5.0	6.3	1.9	7.0	1.8	2.6	1.6	16.8	1.9
Thoroughly rotted	790	145	65.0	5.8	5.0	1.3	8.8	1.8	3.0	1.8	17.0	1.6
Drainage from barn-yard manure	982	7	10.7	1.5	4.9	1.0	0.8	0.4	0.1	0.7	0.2	1.2
Human Fæces, fresh	772	193	29.9	10.0	2.5	1.6	6.2	3.6	10.9	0.8	1.9	0 4
Human Urine, fresh	963	24	13.5	6.0	2.0	4.6	0.2	0.2	1.7	0.4		5.0
Mixed human excrements, fresh	933	51	16.0	7.0	2.1	3.8	0.9	0.6	2.6	0.5	0.2	4.0
Mixed human excrements, mostly liquid	955	30	15.0	3.5	2.0	4 0	1.0	0.6	2.8	0.4	0.2	4.3
Dove manure, fresh	519	308	173.0	17.6	10.0	0.7	16.0	5.0	17.8	3.3	20.2	
Hen manure, fresh	560	255	185.0	16.3	8.5	1.0	24.9	7.4	15.4	4.5	35.2	....
Duck manure, fresh	566	262	172.0	10.0	6.2	0.5	17.0	3.5	14.0	3.5	28.0	......
Geese manure, fresh	771	134	95.0	5.5	9.5	1.3	8.4	2 0	5.4	1.4	14.0	.....
II.—COMMERCIAL MANURES.												
(In 100 parts of Fertilizer.)												
Peruvian Guano	14.8	51.4	33.8	13.0	2.3	1.4	11.0	1.2	13.0	1.0	1.7	1.3
Norway Fish-Guano	12.6	53.4	34.0	9.0	0.3	0.9	15.4	0.6	13·5	0.3	1.6	1.1
Poudrette	24.0	27.0	49.0	2.0	0.9	1.0	18.6	0.5	2.1	1.0	5.4	1.5
Pulverized Dead Animals	5.7	56.9	37.4	6.5	0.3	0.8	18.2	0.4	13.9	1.0	1.7	0.2
Flesh-Meal	27.8	56.6	15.6	9.7			7.0	0.3	6.3	0.1	1.1	......
Dried Blood	14.0	79.0	7.0	11.7	0.7	0.6	0.7	0.1	1.0	0.4	2.1	0.4
Horn-Meal and Shavings	8.5	68.5	25.0	10.2			6.6	9.3	5.5	0.9	11.0	......
Bone-Meal	6.0	33.8	60.7	3.8	0.2	0.3	31.3	1.0	23.2	0.1	8.5	0.3
Bone-Meal from solid parts	5.0	31.5	63.5	3.5	0 1	0.2	33.0	1.0	25.2	0.1	3.0	0.2
Bone-Meal from soft parts	7.0	37.8	55.7	4.0	0.2	0.3	29.0	1.0	20.0	0.1	3.5	0.2

* It is estimated that in the case of horses, cattle and swine, one-third of the urine drains away. The following is the amount of wheat straw used daily as bedding for each animal: Horse, 6 lbs.; Cattle, 8 lbs.; Swine, 4 lbs.; and Sheep, 0.6 lbs.

Name of Fertilizer.	Water.	Organic Substance.	Ash.	Nitrogen.	Potash.	Soda.	Lime.	Magnesia.	Phosphoric Acid.	Sulphuric Acid.	Silica and Sand.	Chlorine & Fluorine
(In 100 parts.)	pr c	pr c	pr c	pr c	pr c	pr c	pr c	pr c	pr c	pr c	pr c	pr c
Bone-black, before used.............	6.0	10.0	84.0	1.0	0.1	0.3	43.0	1.1	32.0	0.4	5.0	
Bone-black, spent......................	10.0	6.0	84.0	0.5	1.1	0.2	37.0	1.1	26.0	0.4	15.0	
Bone-ash.................................	6.0	3.0	91.0		0.3	0.6	46.0	1.2	35.4	0.4	6.5	
Baker Guano...........................	10.0	9.2	81.0	0.5	0.2	1.2	41.5	1.5	34.8	1.5	0.8	0.8
Jarvis Guano............................	11.8	8.2	80.0	0.4	0.4	0.3	39.1	0.5	20.6	18.0	0.5	0.2
Estremadura Apatite................	0.6				0.7	0.3	48.1	0.1	37.6	0.2	9.0	1.5
Sombrero Phosphate................	8.5		91.5	0.1		0.8	43.5	0.6	35.0	0.5	1.0	0.6
Navassa Phosphate..................	2.6	5.4	92.0	0.1			37.5	0.6	33.2	0.5	5.0	0.1
Nassau Phosphorite, rich..........	2.6		97.4		0.8	0.4	45.1	0.2	33.0	0.3	5 5	3.1
Nassau Phosphorite, medium....	2.5		97.5		0.7	0.4	40.1	0.2	24 1		20.8	1.5
Westphalian Phsophorite	6.5	1.6	91.8				21.8	0.9	19.7	1.0	22.0	1.6
Hanover Phosphorite................	2.0	8.5	94.5				37.2	0.2	29.2	0 5	3.3	0.5
Coprolites................................	4.3		95.7		1.0	0.5	45.4	1.0	26.4	0.8	7.5	0.1
Sulphate of Ammonia	4.0			20.0			0 5			58.0	3.0	1.4
Nitrate of Soda.........................	2.6			15.5		35.0	0.2				0.7	1.6	1.7
Wool-dust and offal..................	10.0	56.0	34.0	5.2	0.3	0.1	1.4	0.3	1.3	0.5	29.0	0.2
Common Salt...........................	5.0		95.0			44.3	1.2	0.2		1.4	2.0	48.2
Gypsum or Plaster....................	20.0		80.8				31.0	0.1		44.0	4.0	
Gas-lime..................................	7.0	1.3	91.7	0.4	0.2		64.5	1.5		12.5	3.0	
Sugar-house Scum...................	34.5	24.5	41.0	1.2	0.2	0.6	20 7	0.3	1.5	0.3	9.1	0.1
Leached wood ashes.................	20.0	5.0	75.0		2.5	1.3	24.5	2.5	6.0	0.3	20.0	
Wood-soot...............................	5.0	71.8	23.2	1.3	2.4	0.5	10.0	1.5	0.4	0.3	4.0	
Coal-soot.................................	5.0	70.2	24.8	2.5	0.1		4.0	1.5			1.7	16.0	
Ashes from Deciduous trees......	5.0	5 0	90.0		10.0	2.5	30.0	5.0	6.5	1.6	18.0	0.3
Ashes from Evergreen trees......	5.0	5.0	90.0		6.0	2.0	35.0	6.0	4.5	1.6	18.0	0.8
Peat-ashes...............................	5.0		95.0		1.5	0.8	?	1.5	0.6	1.8	?	0.2
Bituminous coal-ashes..............	5.0		95.0		0.5	6.4	?	3.2	0.2	8.5	?	
Anthracite coal-ashes...............	5.0	5.0	90.0		0.1	0.1	?	8.0	0.1	5.0	?	
III.—SUPERPHOSPHATE, from												
Peruvian Guano.......................	16.0	41.9	42.1	10.0	2.0	1.2	9.5	1.0	10.5	15.0	1.5	1.1
Baker Guano............................	15.0	6.2	78.8	0.3	0.1	0.8	25.9	0.9	21.8	28.5	0.9	0.2
Estremadura Apatite................	15.0		85.0		0.4	0.2	28.2	0.1	22.1	28.5	5.8	0.9
Sombrero Phosphate................	15.0		85.0			0 5	26.4	0.4	20.2	25.8	0.6	0.4
Navassa Phosphate...................	15.0	2.5	82.5			?	17.0	0.3	15.4	19.5	2.3	?
Nassau Phosphorite, rich..........	15.0		85.0	...	0.5	0.2	26.5	0.1	19.4	25.5	3.2	1.3
Nassau Phosphorite, medium....	12.0		88.0		0.3	0.1	24.2	0.1	16.6	19.5	13.5	1.3
Bone-black	15.0	8.0	77.0	0.3		0.1	25.0	0.7	16.2	21.0	9.3	
Bone-Meal................................	13.0	23.8	63.2	2.0	0.1	0.2	22.4	0.7	16.6	19.5	2.5	0.2
Phospho-guano (manufactured)...	15.5	13.0	80.3	8.3	0.3	0.4	24.0		20 5	28.8	3.0	0.9

The following is the analysis of South Carolina Phosphate Rock:

Moisture	1.91
Organic Matter and Water, of combination*........	4.05
Posphoric Acid......................................	26.28
Magnesia...	0.24
Lime	39.78
Potash..	0.20
Soda..	0.63
Chloride Sodium	0.05
Sulphuric Acid......................................	2.50
Oxide of Iron..	1.85
Alumina, and a little Fluorine....................	4.64
Insoluble Silicious matter and Soluble Silica...	15.31
Carbonic Acid.......................................	2.60
	100.00

*Contains, Nitrogen.................0.09
Equal to Ammonia...................0.11

2—. TABLE SHOWING THE DISTRIBUTION OF INGREDIENTS IN SOME MANUFACTURING PROCESSES.

Name of Material.	Dry Substances.	Nitrogen.	Ash.	Potash.	Lime.	Magnesia.	Phosphoric Acid.
1.—BREWING.	lbs	lbs	lbs	lbs	lbs	lbs	lbs
1000 lbs Barley contain..................	855	15.2	22.23	4.48	0.58	1.92	7.71
15 " Hops "	13.2		1.00	0.345	0.167	0.056	0.168
Distribution of the Ingredients:							
Water...............................			1.23	0.852	0.030	0.045	0.234
Malt-Sprouts......................	33	1.38	2.48	0.749	0.69	0.066	0.653
Brewer's Grains..................	260	8.74	13.08	0.580	1.474	1.131	3.631
Spent Hops........................	9		0.54	0.023	0.160	0.055	0.062
Yeast	30	2.94	2.27	0.643	0.097	0.185	1.349
Beer................................		2.14	3.65	1.995		0.484	0.939
2.—DISTILLERY.							
a 1000 lbs Potatoes contain............	250	3.2	9.43	5.69	0.24	0.44	1.63
40 " Kiln-Malt	37	0.56	1.06	0.184	0.040	0.088	0.398
20 " Yeast-Malt	18.5	0.28	0.53	0.092	0.020	0.014	0.194
The Slump contains...................	125	4.04	11.02	5.966	0.300	0.572	2.212
b Grain Spirits.							
800 lbs Rye contain...................	684	14.08	14.32	4.501	0.376	1.648	6.710
200 " Kiln-Malt contain.........	184	2.82	5.12	0.883	0.195	0.420	1.526
50 " Yeast-malt "	46	0.71	1.28	0.221	0.049	0.107	0.382
The Slump, "	443	17.61	20.72	5.605	0.620	2.184	8.618
3.—YEAST MANUFACTURE.							
700 lbs bruised Rye contain	599	12.82	12.53	3.941	0.329	1.444	5.876
300 " Barley-Malt "	276	4.23	7.67	1.325	0.293	0.643	2.801
Distribution of Ingredients:							
Yeast................................	45	4.60	3.41	1.273	0.192	0.867	2.672
Grains and Slump..................	325	11.95	16.79	3.993	0.430	1.720	6.005
4.—STARCH MANUFACTURE.							
1000 lbs Potatoes contain............	250	3.20	9.43	5.69	0.24	0.44	1.63
The remains in the Fibre............	75	0.60	0.54	0.086	0.266	0.042	0.183
The remains in the Water..........	45	2.60	8.89	5.604		0.398	1.497
5.—MILLING.							
1000 lbs Wheat contain	857	20.80	16.88	5.26	0.57	2.02	7.94
Distribution of the Ingredients:							
Flour (77.5 per cent)...............	664	14.65	5.50	1.980	0.154	0.458	2.862
Mill-food (6.5 ")	58	1.64	1.80	0.648	0.050	0.148	0.936
Bran (16.0 ")	135	4.51	9.60	2.672	0.896	1.394	4.102
6.—CHEESE-MAKING.							
1000 lbs milk contain................	125	4.80	6.10	1.505	1.333	0.186	1.735
Distribution of the Ingredients:							
Cheese...............................	65	4.53	2.84	0.247	0.687	0.028	1.151
Whey................................	60	0.27	3.26	1.258	0.646	0.158	0.584
7.—BEET-SUGAR MANUFACTURE.							
1000 lbs Roots contain...............	184	1.60	7.10	3.914	0.379	0.536	0.780
Distribution of the Ingredients:							
Tops and Tails (12 per cent of roots).........	19	0.24	1.15	0.336	0.108	0.132	0.144
Pomace (15 per cent of roots).................	46	0.44	1.71	0.585	0.39	0.105	0.165
Skimmings (4 per cent of roots).....	24	0.60	1.20	0.380	8.640	0.240	0.384
Molasses (3 per cent of roots).................	25	0.32	2.47	1.741	0.141	0.009	0.015
Sugar and loss........	85		0.57	0.872		0.040	0.072
8.—FLAX DRESSING.							
1000 lbs Flax-Stalks contain.........	860		30.36	9.426	6.751	1.995	3.990
Distribution of the Ingredients:							
In the Water........................	215		25.15	9.175	4.100	1.870	34.00
Stems or Husks.....................	460		4.03	0.171	2.052	0.006	0.474
Flax and Tow.......................	155		1.22	0.054	0.648	0.054	0.126

TABLE showing the amount of nitrogen, phosphoric acid, and potash in one ton of the fresh dung and fresh urine of different animals, and also of the drainage of the barn-yard.—*Talks on Manure*—HARRIS.

SUBSTANCE.	1 Ton fresh Dung.			1 Ton fresh Urine.		
	Nitrogen.	Phosphoric Acid.	Potash.	Nitrogen.	Phosphoric Acid.	Potash.
	lbs	lbs	lbs	lbs	lbs	lbs
Horse	8.8	7.0	7.0	31.0		80.0
Cow	5.8	3.4	2.0	11.6		9.8
Sheep	11.0	6.2	3.0	39.0	0.2	45.2
Swine	12.0	8.2	5.2	8.6	1.4	16.6
Mean	9.4	6.2	4.3	22.5	0.4	25.4
Drainage of barnyard				3.0	0.2	9.8

FOODS WHICH MAKE RICH MANURES.

TABLE—Showing the amount of nitrogen, phosphoric acid, and potash in different foods, and the estimated value in ton of manure made from each. Originally prepared by J. B. Lawes, of Rothamstead, England. (Taken from *Talks on Manures—Harris*.)

SUBSTANCE.	PER CENT.					Value of manure in dollars and cents, from one ton (2,000 lbs.) of food.
	Total dry matter.	Total mineral matter (ash).	Phosphoric acid reckoned as phosphate of lime.	Potash.	Nitrogen.	
Linseed Cake	88.0	7.00	4.92	1.65	4.75	$ 19 72
Cotton Seed Cake	89.0	8.00	7.00	3.12	6.50	27 86
Rape Cake	89.0	8.00	5.75	1.76	5.00	21 01
Linseed	90.0	4.00	3.38	1.87	3.80	15 65
Beans	84.0	3.00	2.20	1.27	4.00	15 75
Peas	84.5	2.40	1.84	0.96	3.40	18 38
Tares	84.0	2.00	1.68	0.66	4 20	16 75
Lentils	88.0	3.00	1.89	0.96	4.30	16 51
Malt-dust	94.0	8.50	5.23	2.12	4.20	18 21
India Meal	89.0	1.80	1.18	0.35	1.80	6 65
Wheat	85.0	1.70	1.87	0.50	1.80	7 08
Barley	84.0	2.20	1.35	0.55	1.65	6 82
Malt	95.0	2.60	1.60	0.65	1 70	6 65
Oats	86.0	2.85	1.17	0.50	2.00	7 70
*Fine Pollard	86.0	5.60	6.44	1.46	2.60	13 58
†Coarse Pollard	86.0	6.20	7.52	1.49	2.58	14 86
Wheat-bran	86.0	6.60	7.95	1.45	2.55	14 59
Clover Hay	84.0	7.50	1.25	1.30	2.10	9 64
Meadow Hay	84.0	6.00	0.88	1.50	1.50	6 48
Bean Straw	82.5	5.55	0.90	1.11	0.90	3 87
Pea Straw	82.0	5.95	0.85	0.89		8 74
Wheat Straw	84.0	5.60	0.55	0.05	0.00	2 68
Barley Straw	85.0	4.50	0.37	0.68	0·50	2 25
Oat Straw	83.0	5.50	0.48	0.93	0.60	2 90
Mangel Wurzel	12.5	1.00	0.09	0.25	0.25	1 07
Swedish Turnips	11.0	.68	0.13	0.22	0.22	91
Common Turnips	8.0	.68	0.11	0.18	0.18	86
Potatoes (Irish)	24.0	1.00	0.32	0.35	0.35	1 50
Carrots	13.5	.70	0.13	0.20	0.20	80
Parsnips	15.0	1.00	0.42	0.22	0.22	1 14

*Middlings.
†Shipstuff.

THE COTTON PLANT AND ITS PRODUCTS.

The fact nas been thoroughly and practically demonstrated that by a careful husbanding of home manures, three-fourths of the money usually expended in the purchase of commercial fertilizers may be retained in the pockets of the farmers without any diminution of the crops produced.

Yet, while spending their hard-earned money for commercial fertilizers, they are guilty of the most extravagant waste of these home materials. There is no country in the world more fruitful in the production of home manures than one in which cotton is the staple product; nor is there any in which so little plant-food is sold from the farm. On a farm on which cotton is the staple product, only 2¾ pounds of plant food are sold from the average Georgia acre, while 97 are returned to the soil in the plant and the seed, as shown by the following analysis of the cotton plant by H. C. White, Professor of Chemistry in the University of Georgia:

Under the head of

"THE CHEMISTRY OF THE COTTON PLANT,"

Prof. White says: "The cotton plant, as it stands in the field ripened and ready for picking, may be divided into six parts: the lint, seed, bolls, leaves, stem and roots. An average plant, air dried, may be assumed to weigh 3.5 ounces.* Of this:

The lint will weigh..................................0.3 ounces.
The seed will weigh................................0.6 ounces.
The bolls will weigh...............................0.5 ounces.
The leaves will weigh..............................0.5 ounces.
The stem will weigh................................1.3 ounces.
The roots will weigh...............................0.3 ounces.

"In producing an average crop of 150 pounds of lint cotton per acre, there will have been grown on the acre 150 pounds lint, 300 pounds seed, 250 pounds bolls, 250 pounds leaves, 600 pounds stem, and 150 pounds roots.

	Organic matter.	Mineral matter or ash.
The lint consists of, (in 100 parts)....	98.25.................	1.75
The seed consists of (in 100 parts)...	96.59....	3.41
The bolls consists of, (in 100 parts) ..	85.24.................	12.96
The leaves consists of, (in 100 parts).	82.74.................	15.22
The stem consists of, (in 100 parts)...	95.02.................	3.98
The roots consists of, (in 100 parts)..	92.76.................	5.08

"The organic matter consists, in all cases, of oxygen, hydrogen,

---

*An average obtained by actually weighing a number of plants carefully air dried; such as would probably produce the assumed average crop of 150 pounds per acre.

carbon and nitrogen. The different portions of the plant contain in 100 parts the following respective amounts of nitrogen:

```
Lint..................................................0.54
Seed .................................................1.96
Bolls.................................................1.03
Leaves................................................2.14
Stem..................................................1.16
Roots.................................................1.17
```

"The ash of the lint will contain in 100 parts

```
Phosphoric acid......................................10.25
Potash...............................................21.34
Lime.................................................26.74
Magnesia............................................. 9.46
Other mineral matter.................................32.21
```

"There will be contained in one hundred parts of the ash of

	Seed.	Bolls.	Leaves.	Stem.	Roots.
Phosphoric acid	35.76	6.87	7.75	13.68	7.50
Potash	30.25	14.28	14.96	24.06	23.52
Lime	9.87	27.31	28.14	26.36	23.37
Magnesia	12.42	6.14	6.11	9.75	8.23
Sulphuric acid	6.48	13.25	12.97	5.52	4.12
Oxide of iron	1.87	5.12	5.60	1.41	6.98
Chlorine	.85	4.11	4.65	6.42	8.01
Soda	2.50	8.84	9.25	6.79	10.64
Silica	—	14.08	10.57	7.01	8.63

"In reviewing these results, we observe that the most important mineral constituents in each and every part of the cotton plant are phosphoric acid, potash, lime and magnesia. In round numbers, we have in 100 parts of the ash of each part of the plant, the following amounts of these main constituents:

"In 100 of the ash of

	Lint.	Seed.	Bolls.	Leaves.	Stem.	Roots.
Phosphoric acid	10	36	7	8	14	8
Potash	21	30	14	15	24	.24
Lime	27	10	27	28	26	22
Magnesia	10	12	6	6	10	8

"Estimated from these per centages and the proportion of ash before stated, as yielded by the several parts of the plant, we have in 100 parts:

	Lint.	Seed.	Boll.	Leaves.	Stem.	Root.
Phosphoric acid	0.18	1.22	.91	1.22	.56	.40
Potash	0.37	1.02	1.82	3.28	.96	1.22
Lime	0.48	.34	3.49	4.25	1.04	1.12
Magnesia	0.17	.41	.77	.92	.40	.41
Nitrogen	0.54	1.96	1.03	2.14	1.16	1.17

"As before stated, in producing an average crop of 150 pounds of lint cotton per acre, there will also have been produced 300 pounds seed, 250 pounds bolls, 250 pounds leaves, 600 pounds stems and 150 pounds roots.

"There will be contained in

	150 lbs. lint	300 lbs. seed	250 lbs. bolls	250 lbs. leaves	600 lbs. stems	150 lbs. roots
Pounds phosphoric acid	0.27	3 66	2.26	3.05	3 36	0.60
Pounds potash	0.54	3.06	4.52	8.20	5 76	1.83
Pounds lime	0.72	1.02	8.82	10 60	6.24	1.68
Pounds magnesia	0.24	1.23	1.93	2.30	2.40	0.61
Pounds nitrogen	0.81	5.88	5.07	5.35	6 96	1.75

"To sum up, therefore, we find that to produce the above stated average crop of lint cotton per acre, there would be required in all:

Phosphoric acid..13 pounds.
Potash..21 pounds.
Lime..80 pounds.
Magnesia..9 pounds.
Nitrogen..26 pounds.

"The bolls, leaves, stem and roots are usually returned at once to the soil, and with them is returned in round numbers:

Phosphoric acid..............9 pounds....Magnesia................7 pounds.
Potash.....................20 pounds....Nitrogen............... 19 pounds.
Lime...................... 27 pounds.

"Of the remainder, there is left in the gin-house, with the seed:

Phosphoric acid..............4 pounds....Magnesia................1 pound.
Potash......................3 pounds....Nitrogen................6 pounds.
Lime.......................1 pound.

"Whilst there is entirely removed from the acre, and sent into market with the lint:

Phosphoric acid..............¼ pound....Magnesia........ ....¼ pound.
Potash......................¼ pound....Nitrogen................1 pound."
Lime.......................¾ pound.

Let us now examine the analyses of one of the principal cereals and see how the quantity of plant-food removed in this from an average acre of land compares with the above.

Since a larger proportion of the grain of wheat is removed from the farm than of any other cereal, it will best illustrate the point in hand. As the straw and chaff are generally returned in some form to the soil, they are omitted in the calculation of the quantity of plant-food removed from the farm.

Assuming ten bushels as the average yield per acre—a fair assumption for grain growing regions—a calculation on that basis from analysis of Wolff and Knop shows the following quantities of the principal elements of plant-food are removed in every ten bushels of wheat sold from the farm, compared with that removed in lint from an average acre in cotton :

	Wheat.	Lint cotton.
Nitrogen	12.40 pounds	1.00 pounds.
Potash	3.30 pounds	.50 pounds.
Lime	.36 pounds	.75 pounds.
Magnesia	1.40 pounds	.25 pounds.
Phosphoric acid	4.90 pounds	.25 pounds.
Total	32.36 pounds	2.75 pounds.

This represents a most remarkable contrast between the exhausting effects of wheat and cotton in the amounts of the elements of plant food removed by sale from the soil, and yet the cotton soils are being more rapidly exhausted than those on which wheat is the principal staple produced for market.

These seem to be contradictory facts which demand explanation.

The apparent contradiction arises from the existence of other factors which are operative to a greater extent in aid of exhaustion on the cotton than on the wheat farm.

In wheat growing regions the soil is not denuded of vegetable matter during the leaching rains of winter and spring, but is protected, either by small grain or grass, from surface washing.

The summer fallow, in the preparation for seeding wheat, necessarily returns more or less vegetable matter to the soil, and with it not only mineral elements of plant-food, derived from the soil in an available form, thus returning, in an improved condition, all that the plants turned under have taken from the soil, but this return is augmented by whatever organic matter the plants have extracted from the atmosphere. Not only are more stock kept, and consequently more animal manure produced, but more attention given to its collection, and more care taken to protect it from the injurious effects of leaching and evaporation. It will thus be observed that while much plant-food is removed in the produce sent to market, but little is wasted of the natural manurial resources of the farm.

On the cotton farm, the fields are left bare after the crops are gathered, and exposed throughout the winter to leaching and washing action of the rainy season. A single heavy rain in winter or early spring, when the surface is finely pulverized by recent freezes, often causes greater injury to the naked fields of the South than would the removal of a dozen crops of lint cotton. This could be prevented by sowing oats or rye at the last plowing of the cotton, or in August or first of September, even *without plowing* them in, leaving them to germinate under the influence of the equinoctial rains. These would serve the double purpose of protecting the land from waste during the winter, and of furnishing a green crop to be turned under in the preparation of the soil for the spring crops. The denudation of soils of vegetable matter, by clean culture and the absence of any system of rotation of crops, is a fruitful source of the rapid exhaustion of Georgia soils. The waste of natural manurial agencies on Southern farms is without a parallel. Cotton seed are "thrown out to rot," where they are robbed alternately by the leaching rains and the drying winds, until much of the soluble plant-food is lost. Mules and cattle are fed in unsheltered lots, where fully one-half of the soluble parts of their manure is washed into the adjacent streams or passes off into the air under the influence of the winds and the sun.

Cotton farms, therefore, have not been exhausted by the removal of plant-foot in the sale of their products, but by exposure to winter rains, by the waste of home manurial resources, and the absence of a system of rotation by which the soil is supplied, periodically, with a sufficiency of vegetable matter.

It is gratifying to be able to say that there is a growing disposition to adopt a more rational and self-sustaining system of farm economy. Home manures are being more carefully husbanded and the compost system being generally adopted, as recommended in the circulars of the Department.

COMPOSTING SUPERPHOSPHATES WITH HOME MANURES.

When we consider the fact that the farmers of Georgia expended about *four millions* dollars last season for fertilizers, even on a cash basis, the question of the most economical mode of permanently improving our soils, and at the same time producing remunerative crops, is one of vital importance to our people.

The Philosophy of Composting.—Stable manure is admitted on all sides to be a complete manure, in the sense of containing all of the necessary elements of plant-food. There are some of the more important elements (phosphoric acid is the principal) which are contained in such small percentage, that large quantities of the manure must be applied in order to secure a sufficient quantity of this essential element for the necessities of plant sustenance. To supply this deficiency, superphosphate is added to the compost heap. A combination of stable manure and cotton seed, in the proportions recommended, supplies enough ammonia for summer crops, but hardly sufficient for winter small grain, unless applied at the rate of 400 pounds per acre. The sulphate of lime contained in every superphosphate, besides being otherwise valuable as a chemical agent, serves to fix the ammonia generated in the progress of decomposition in the compost heap. The fermentation reduces the coarse material, and prepares it for the use of the plant.

"*Composting in the Ground.*"—This is advocated by Prof. Pendleton and others, and as far as results on crops are concerned, is satisfactory, but has some serious objections in practice. If cotton seed are used, they must be put into the ground before warm weather commences, to prevent germination. This necessitates stirring the manure just before planting, which would risk bringing some of it to the surface, or the crop must be planted on a hard bed. Another difficulty under the general practice in Middle and Southern Georgia, is that stock would have to be taken out of the field before spring. This would be advantageous to the land, but would give the planter some inconvenience. There is no labor saved by this system, but it is applied at a season of comparative leisure.

Composting Under Shelter.—This may usually be done on rainy days, or when the ground is too wet for the plow, so that little time need be lost by the manipulation of the heap. There are two methods practiced with equally satisfactory results:

One is to apply the different ingredients in successive layers, and cut down vertically after a thorough fermentation has taken place, mixing well with the shovel at the same time.

The other is to mix thoroughly the ingredients at first, and allow the mass to stand until used.

The effects of composts thus prepared far exceed the indications of analysis, and, cost considered, are truly remarkable.

Formulæ for Composting.—If the stable manure and cotton seed have been preserved under shelter, use the following:

FORMULA NO. 1.

Stable Manure..650 lbs.
Cotton Seed (green)..650 lbs.
Superphosphate..700 lbs.

Making a ton of..2,000 lbs.

Directions for Composting.—Spread under shelter a layer of stable manure four inches thick; on this sprinkle a portion of the phosphate; next spread a layer of cotton seed three inches thick; wet these thoroughly with water, and then apply more of the phosphate; next spread another layer of stable manure *three* inches thick, and continue to repeat these layers in the above order, and in proportion to the quantity of each used to the ton, until the material is consumed. Cover the whole mass with stable manure, or scrapings from the lot one or two inches thick. Allow the heap to stand in this condition until a thorough fermentation takes place, which will require from three to six weeks, according to circumstances, dependent upon proper degree of moisture, and the strength of the materials used. When the cotton seed are thoroughly killed, with a sharp hoe, or mattock, cut down vertically through the layers; pulverize and shovel into a heap, where the fermentation will be renewed, and the compost be still further improved. Let it lie two weeks after cutting down; it will then be ready for use.

The following plan of mixing, gives equally satisfactory results: Mix the cotton seed and the stable manure in proper proportion, moisten them with water, apply the proper proportion of phosphate, and mix thoroughly, shoveling into a mass as prepared.

There is some advantage in this plan, from the fact that the ingredients are thoroughly commingled during fermentation.

FOR COTTON.—Apply in the opening furrow 200 pounds, and with the planting seed 75 or 100 pounds, making in all 275 or 300 pound per acre. If it is desired to apply a larger quantity, open furrows the desired distance, and over them sow, broadcast, 400 pounds per acre; bed the land, and then apply 100 pounds per acre with the seed.

FOR CORN.—Apply in the hill, by the side of the seed, one gill to the hill. An additional application around the stalk, before the first plowing, will largely increase the yield of grain.

If the compost is to be used on worn, or sandy pine lands, use the following:

FORMULA NO. 2.

Stable Manure..600 lbs.
Cotton Seed (green)..600 lbs.
Superphosphate..700 lbs.
Kainit..100 lbs.

Making a ton of..2,000 lbs.

Prepare as directed for No. 1, moistening the manure and cotton seed with a solution of the kainit instead of water. Muriate of potash is the cheapest form in which potash can be used, but kainit supplies it in a better form and combination for many plants.

If lot manure, or that which has been so exposed as to lose some of its fertilizing properties, is composted, use—

FORMULA NO. 3.

Lot Manure	600 lbs.
Cotton Seed (green)	500 lbs.
Superphosphate	700 lbs.
Sulphate of Ammonia	60 lbs.
Kainit	140 lbs.
Making a ton of	2,000 lbs.

The sulphate of ammonia and kainit must be dissolved in warm water, and a proportionate part of each sprinkled upon the other ingredients as the heap is prepared. Apply as directed under No. 1, to cotton and corn. To wheat or oats, apply 400 or 500 pounds per acre, broadcast, and plow or harrow it in with the grain.

SOME USEFUL TABLES

WEIGHTS AND MEASURES.

One bushel of	lbs.	One bushel of	lbs.
Wheat weighs	60	Salt weighs	55
Corn, shelled, weighs	56	Bran weighs	20
Corn, in the ear, weighs	70	Turnips weighs	55
Corn-meal weighs	48	Ground peas	24
Peas weighs	60	Cotton seed weighs	30
Rye weighs	56	Buckwheat wheat	52
Oats weighs	32	Clover seed weighs	60
Barley weighs	47	Timothy seed weighs	45
Irish potatoes weighs	60	Flax seed weighs	58
Sweet potatoes weighs	55	Blue grass seed weighs	14
Dried apples weighs	24	Millet seed weighs	50
Dried peaches weighs	33	Hungarian grass seed weighs	54
Onions weighs	57	Orchard grass seed weighs	14

A box 24x16 inches, 52 inches deep, contains............one barrel
A box 16x16$\frac{8}{10}$ inches, 8 inches deep, contains............one bushel
A box 8x8$\frac{8}{10}$ inches, 8 inches deep, contains............one peck
A box 4x4 inches, 4$\frac{1}{2}$ inches deep, contains............half peck
A box 4x4 inches, 1$\frac{1}{2}$ inches deep, contains............one quart

U. S. standard bushel, or Winchester bushel, contains 2150.42 cubic inches. Its dimensions are 18$\frac{1}{2}$ inches in diameter inside, and 8 inches deep.

Table showing proper age for reproduction, period of gestation, incubation, &c., of different animals.

KINDS OF ANIMALS.	Proper age for reproduction.	Period of the power of reproduction.	Number of females for one male.	Period of gestation and incubation.		
				Shortest period.	Mean period.	Longest period.
	Years.	Years.		Days.	Days.	Days.
Mare	4 years.	10 to 12		322	347	419
Stallion	5 years.	12 to 15	20 to 30			
Cow	3 years.	10		240	283	321
Bull	3 years.	5	30 to 40			
Ewe	2 years.	6		146	154	161
Buck	2 years.	7	40 to 50			
Sow	1 year.	6		109	115	143
Boar	1 year.	6	6 to 10			
She-Goat	2 years.	6		150	156	163
He-Goat	2 years.	5	20 to 40			
She-Ass	4 years.	10 to 12		365	380	391
He-Ass	5 years.	12 to 15				
She-Buffalo				281	308	335
Bitch	2 years.	8 to 9		55	60	63
Dog	2 years.	8 to 9				
She-Cat	1 year.	5 to 6		48	50	56
He-Cat	1 year.	9 to 10	5 to 6			
Doe-Rabbit	6 months.	5 to 6		20	28	35
Buck-Rabbit	6 months.	5 to 6	30			
Cock	6 months.	5 to 6	12 to 15			
Turkey, sitting on the eggs of the			{ Hen	17	24	28
			{ Duck	24	27	30
			{ Turkey	24	26	30
Hen, sitting on the eggs of the			{ Duck	26	30	34
			{ Hen	19	21	24
Duck		8 to 5		28	30	32
Goose				27	30	33
Pigeon				16	18	20

Number of plants or trees that can be planted on an acre of ground, at the following distances apart in feet:

DISTANCES APART.	NO. OF PLANTS.	DISTANCES APART.	NO. OF PLANTS.
1 by 1	43,560	7 by 7	888
1½ by 1½	19,360	8 by 8	680
2 by 1	21,780	9 by 9	537
2 by 2	10,890	10 by 10	435
2½ by 2½	6,969	11 by 11	360
3 by 1	15,520	12 by 12	302
3 by 2	7,260	13 by 13	257
3 by 3	4,840	14 by 14	222
3½ by 3½	3,555	15 by 15	193
4 by 1	10,890	16 by 16	170
4 by 2	5,445	17 by 17	150
4 by 3	3,630	18 by 18	134
4 by 4	2,722	19 by 19	120
4½ by 4½	2,151	20 by 20	108
5 by 1	8,712	24 by 24	75
5 by 2	4,356	25 by 25	69
5 by 3	2,904	27 by 27	59
5 by 4	2,178	30 by 30	48
5 by 5	1,742	40 by 40	27
5½ by 5½	1,417	50 by 50	17
6 by 6	1,210	60 by 60	12
6½ by 6½	1,031	66 by 66	10

Multiply the distances into each other, and divide it by the square feet in an acre, or 43,560, and the quotient is the number of plants.— *Rural Affairs.*

INDEX.

A.

Acid 8
Acid—Carbonic 15
Acid—Sulphuric 20
Acid—Acetic 62
Acid—Phosphoric 23
Acids—Vegetable. 61
Agricultural Experiments 114
Albumen—Vegetable 64
Albumen—Animal 63
Albuminoids 63, 65, 66, 109
Albuminoids and Carbo-hydrates, ratio
 of, etc 110
Alcohol 61
Alkaline Earths 8
Alumina 28
Aluminum 28
Alum 29
Ammonia 13
Analysis ....7—92
Analysis—quantitative 8
Analysis—qualitative 8
Analysis of agricultural plants 57
Animal products 155
Animal manures—Composition of 159
Anther 51
Appendix 151
Ash elements and their compounds ...67, 74,
 75, 88, 89.
Assimilation 48
Atmosphere and plants—Relation be-
 tween 57
Atmosphere in its relations to vegetation 80

B.

Barium 32
Bedding—Materials for 154
Beetles 144
Bone ash 22
Bone black 14
Bones—Composition of 21
Botany 5
Bromine 32
Butterflies 146, 148

C.

Calcium 26
Cane Sugar 60
Carbon 13
Carbonic Acid 15, 82
Carbonate of Soda 26
Carbonate of Lime 26, 27
Carbonic Acid—imbibed by leaves 55
Carbo-hydrates 58
Case-hardening 80
Caseine 64
Caustic Lime 26
Cell walls 46
Cellulose 46, 58, 59
Charleston Phosphate 21
Chemistry 5, 9
Chemistry—Organic 9
Chemistry—Inorganic 9
Chemical composition of plants 55
Chemical agents 75
Chemical Analysis 87
Chemical symbols 6, 7
Chemical compounds 8
Chloride of Lime 28
Chlorine 29
Chloride of Potassium 24
Chilian Saltpetre 26
Chromium 32
Chaff 154
Circulation of sap 53
Citric Acid 61
Climate—Influence of 96
Cobalt 32
Coleoptera 144
Combustion 17
Composts 77
Composting Super-phosphate with home
 manures 164
Composting—Formula for 165
Composting—Directions for 165, 166
Copper 32
Corundum 28
Corn 95, 112
Cotton 94
Cotton fibre 89
Cotton seed 77, 89, 106
Cotton plant and its products 160
Cotton plant—Chemistry of 160

D.

Definition of Terms 5
Dextrine 59
Dicotyledons 38
Diptera 149
Directions for Composting 165
Drainage—Effects of 91
Drainage 121
Drainage—Where necessary 122
Drainage—What it does 124
Drainage—Where to begin 128
Drainage—Material for 128
Drains—Different kinds 128, 131
Dried blood 99

E.

Earths—Alkaline 8
Elements—List of 7
Element 5
Endogens 38, 45
Endosmose 41
Entomology 5
Entomology—In its relations to agricul-
 ture 143
Entomology—Science of 144
Epsom Salts 20
Essential organs 52
Evaporation—Effects of 140
Excrement 98
Exhalation from plants 82
Experiment 7
Experiments—Laboratory 115
Experiments—Field 115
Experiments—List of 116
Exosmose 41
Exogens 38, 45, 46
Exposure—Influence of 144

INDEX.

F.

Farmyard manure 74
Fermentation 18
Fertilizers 97
Fertilizing agents 98
Fertilizers—Mineral 99
Fertilizers—Vegetable 101
Fertilizers—Commercial 106
Fish scrap 98
Flower buds 44
Fodder—Green 152
Foods which make rich manure 159
Formulæ for composting 165
Frost—Influence of 140
Fruit sugar 60

G.

General Chemistry 5
Geology 5
Gestation—Period of 168
Glauber salts 20
Gluten 64
Grape Sugar 60
Grasshoppers 145
Grains and seeds 154
Gums 59
Gypsum 20, 28, 103

H.

Hawk-moths 148
Hay 152
Hemenoptera 148
Hemiptera 146
Humus 15, 78
Hydrogen 10

I.

Imbibition 53
Incubation—Period of 168
Inorganic Chemistry 9
Introductory 3
Iron 29
Iron—Cast 30
Iron—Wrought 30
Iron—Galvanized 31
Iron—Pyrites 31
Iron—Sulphate of 31
Irrigation 135

K.

Kainit 24

L.

Lead 32
Lead—Sugar of 33
Leaf buds 44
Leaves 48
Leaves—Exhalation from 49
Leaves and stems of root crops 153
Legumes 105
Lepodoptera 146
Lignin 59
Lime 26, 76, 77, 78, 79, 101
Lime—Carbonate of 102
Lime—Air-slaked 102
Lime—Sulphate of 103
Litharge 33

M.

Magnesium 28
Magnesia 28, 104

Manganese 33
Malic Acid 61
Marls 27
Manures—Composition of 156
Manures—Composition of Animal 159
Manures—Foods which make rich 159
Manufactured products and refuse 153
Manufacturing processes—Ingredients in 158
Mechanical agents 78
Meteorology 5, 137
Mercury 33
Milk Sugar 60
Mineralogy 5
Mineral Waters 31
Mineral Plant-food 87
Mineral Elements 88
Mineral Fertilizers 99
Mixture 8
Moths 146, 148
Monocotyledons 38
Muck 15, 105

N.

Neuroptera 146
Nickel 33
Nitrates 12
Nitrate of Potash 25
Nitrate of Soda 100
Nitrogen 12, 107

O.

Oats 95, 112
Object of the work 4
Ochre—Red or yellow 29
Oils—Vegetable 62
Organic Chemistry 9
Organs of vegetation 50
Organs of reproduction 50
Organic substances 55, 56
Orthoptera 145
Osmose 40
Ovary 52
Ovule 52
Oxalic Acid 62
Oxygen 9, 18

P.

Paris Green 31
Peas 95
Peat 14
Petrified wood 23
Pistils 51, 52
Phosphorus 20
Phosphoric Acid 21, 89, 94, 100
Phosphoric Acid—Soluble 22
Phosphoric Acid—Insoluble 22
Phosphoric Acid—Precipitated 22, 23
Phosphoric Acid—Available 23
Phosphate of Lime 28
Plaster of Paris 28
Platinum 33
Plants—Chemistry of 154
Plants—On an acre 168
Plants—Structure and office of different parts 34
Plants—Decotyledonous 38
Plants—Exogenous 38
Plants—Monocotyledonous 38
Plants—Polycotyledonous 39
Plant fertilization .... 67 to 72
Plants as food for animals 108
Plant food 73
Polycotyledons 39
Pollen 51

Potash..................................24, 89, 100
Potash—Nitrate of.........................25, 101
Potash—Carbonate of.........................101
Potash—Sulphate of..........................101
Potassium....................................24
Potassium—Chloride of.......................101
Protoplasm...................................46
Proximate principles—Table of...............110
Prussic Acid.................................62
Pole drains.................................128

R.

Reproduction—Proper age for in animals...168
Rock salt....................................25
Roots......................34, 35, 36, 87, 40
Root caps................................35, 152
Root hairs...................................39
Root pruning.................................43
Root development—When most active............42
Roots and stems—Correspondence between.......................................42

S.

Salt.................................19, 25, 100
Salt springs.................................25
Sand...23
Sap—Circulation of...........................53
Scheel's Green...............................31
Seeds—Temperature at which they germinate...................................141
Seeds and grains............................154
Silicon......................................23
Silica.......................................23
Silver.......................................23
Spongeoles...................................35
Soda....................................25, 100
Soda—Nitrate of.........................25, 100
Soda—Bicarbonate of..........................26
Sodium.......................................25
Sodium—Chloride of...........................25
Soil fertilizatoin...........................72
Soil water...................................22
Soil exhaustion..............................93
Soils—their relation to vegetation...........72
Soils—Sedentary..............................83
Soils—Transported............................83
Soils—Drift..................................83
Soils—Alluvial...............................84
Soils—Colluvial..............................84
Soils—Classification of......................84
Soils—Clay...................................85
Soils—Color and texture of...................86
Soils—Capacity for heat.....................141
Stamens......................................51

Starch...................................58, 59
Steel..80
Stems..43
Stigma.......................................52
Style..52
Straw.......................................153
Sugars.......................................59
Sugar-Cane...................................89
Sugar—Grape..................................60
Sugar—Fruit..................................60
Sugar—Milk...................................60
Sugar of Lead................................33
Sulphur......................................19
Sulphuric Acid...............................20
Sulphate of Lime.............................20
Sulphate of Magnesia.........................20
Sulphate of Soda.........................20, 26
Sulphate of Ammonia..........................20
Sulphate of Potash...........................20
Sulphate of Iron.............................31
Superphosphate of Lime.......................22
Symbols—Chemical..........................6, 7

T.

Table for calculating the exhaustion and enriching of soils.......................152
Tables of weights and measures..............167
Tanic Acid...................................62
Tartaric Acid................................61
Tiles.......................................133
Tin..33
Tobacco......................................89
Tree Rock....................................23

V.

Vegetable acids..............................61
Vegetable fibrin.............................64
Vegetable casiene............................64
Verdigris....................................32
Vinegar......................................62
Vitriol—Oil of...............................20
Vitriols.....................................20

W.

Water..11
Water—in fresh plants........................54
Water—in air dry plants......................54
Welding......................................30
Weights and Measures........................107
Wheat....................................89, 95

Z.

Zinc...34
Zoology.......................................5

www.ingramcontent.com/pod-product-compliance
Lightning Source LLC
Chambersburg PA
CBHW022116160426
43197CB00009B/1051